Fun and Simple Origami

101 Easy-to-Fold Projects

Other books by John Montroll:

Origami and Math Simple to Complex

Dinosaur Origami

Origami Dinosaurs for Beginners

Mythological Creatures and the Chinese Zodiac Origami

Origami Worldwide

Origami Under the Sea by John Montroll and Robert J. Lang

Sea Creatures in Origami by John Montroll and Robert J. Lang

Teach Yourself Origami Second Revised Edition

Bringing Origami to Life

Dollar Bill Animals in Origami

Bugs and Birds in Origami

Dollar Bill Origami

Classic Polyhedra Origami

A Constellation of Origami Polyhedra

Christmas Origami

Storytime Origami

Super Simple Origami

Easy Dollar Bill Origami

Fun and Simple Origami

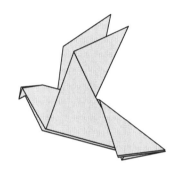

101 Easy-to-Fold Projects

John Montroll

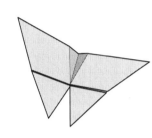

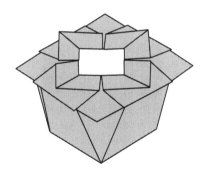

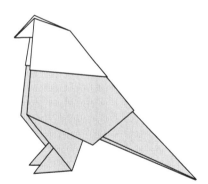

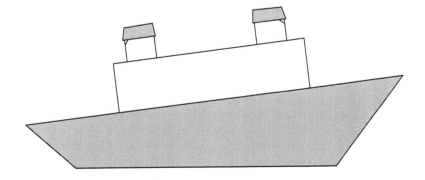

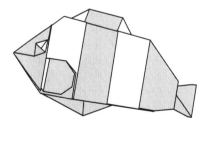

To Gil, Aliza, and Simcha

Fun and Simple Origami

ISBN-10: 1478189835
ISBN-13: 978-1478189831

Introduction

Origami is a fascinating art. Here is a large collection of mostly simple, traditional models. Many topics are covered including birds, boats, boxes, and more. Children can fold from a wide variety and others can use this volume to teach classes and origami workshops.

You can fold a collection of hats, boats, objects, birds, fish, animals, and more. Clear diagrams show how to fold some kimonos, a pagoda, flying bird, Chinese Vase, and many more. Most are traditional and a few are my designs or variations of traditional models. The models are kept at a simple level.

The diagrams are drawn in the internationally approved Randlett–Yoshizawa style, which is easy to follow once you have learned the basic folds. You can use any kind of square paper for these models, but the best results can be achieved using standard origami paper, which is colored on one side and white on the other. In these diagrams, the shading represents the colored side. Origami paper can be found in many hobby shops or on several online sites including www.origami-usa.org.

I hope you enjoy this large collection and wish to continue to discover more.

John Montroll
www.johnmontroll.com

Contents

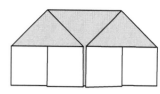

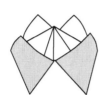

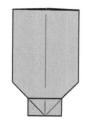

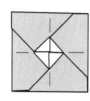
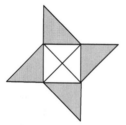

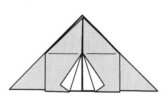
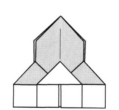

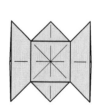
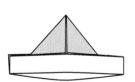
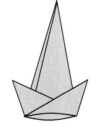

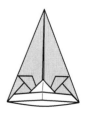

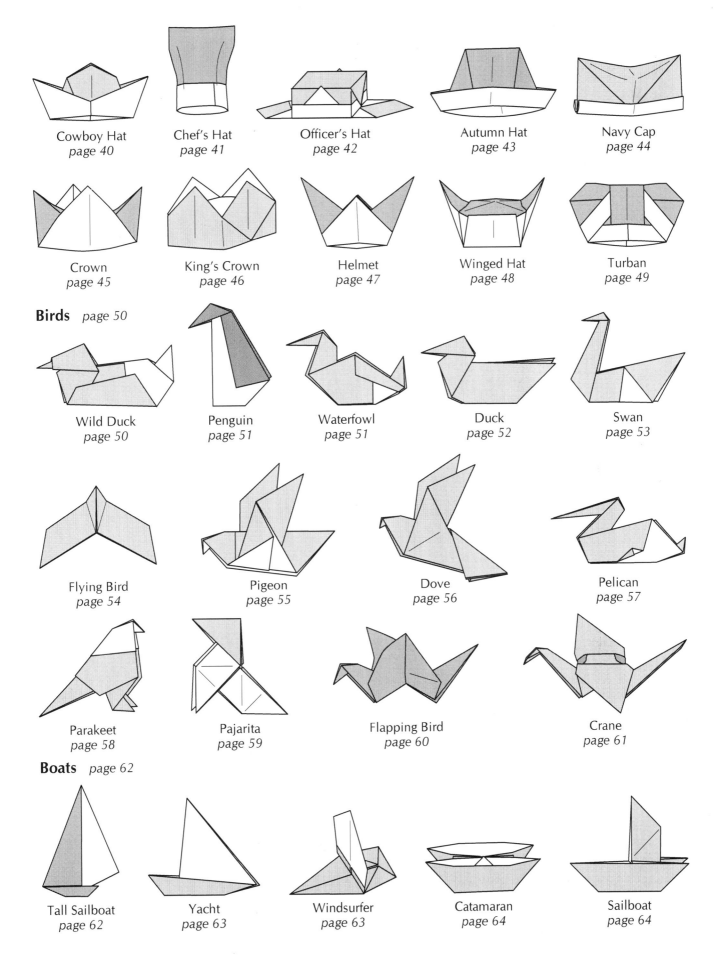

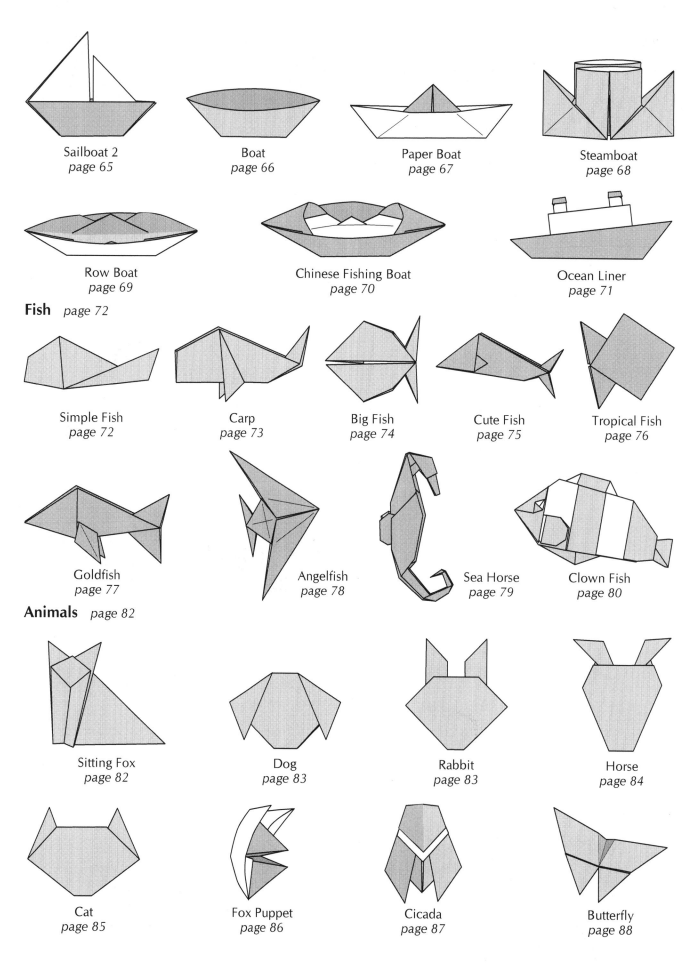

Sailboat 2
page 65

Boat
page 66

Paper Boat
page 67

Steamboat
page 68

Row Boat
page 69

Chinese Fishing Boat
page 70

Ocean Liner
page 71

Fish   *page 72*

Simple Fish
page 72

Carp
page 73

Big Fish
page 74

Cute Fish
page 75

Tropical Fish
page 76

Goldfish
page 77

Angelfish
page 78

Sea Horse
page 79

Clown Fish
page 80

Animals   *page 82*

Sitting Fox
page 82

Dog
page 83

Rabbit
page 83

Horse
page 84

Cat
page 85

Fox Puppet
page 86

Cicada
page 87

Butterfly
page 88

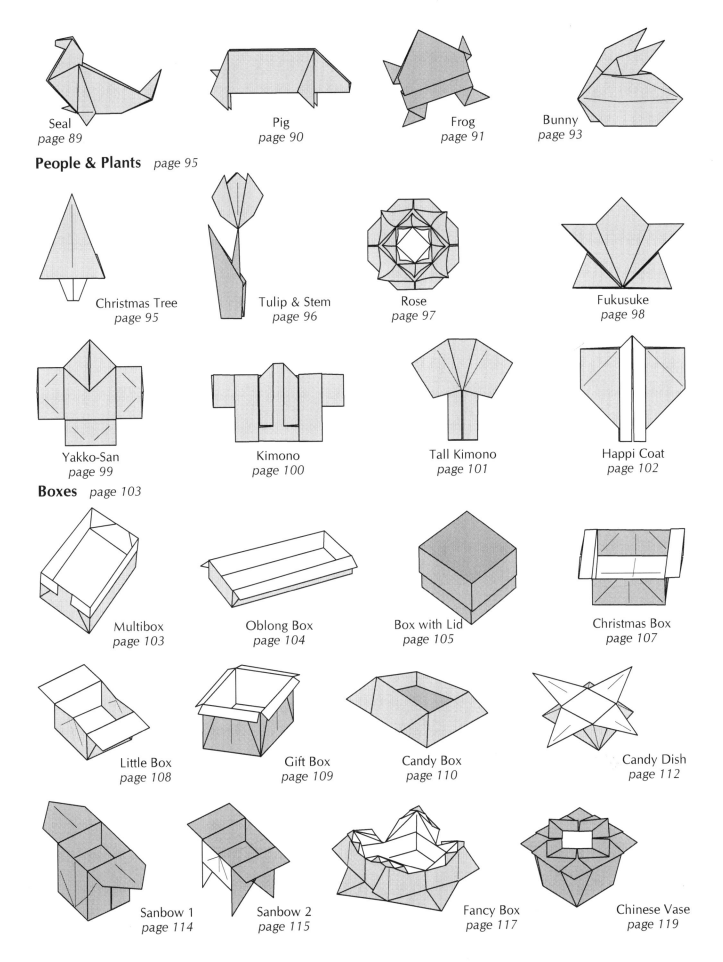

Symbols

Lines

— — — — — — — —   Valley fold, fold in front.

— ·· — ·· — ·· — ·· — ·· —   Mountain fold, fold behind.

———————————   Crease line.

···   X-ray or guide line.

Arrows

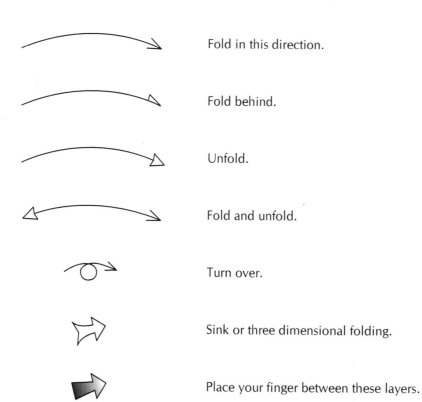

Fold in this direction.

Fold behind.

Unfold.

Fold and unfold.

Turn over.

Sink or three dimensional folding.

Place your finger between these layers.

Basic Folds

Squash Fold.

In a squash fold, some paper is opened and then made flat. The shaded arrow shows where to place your finger.

1
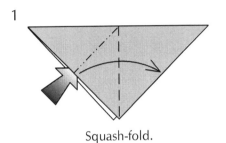
Squash-fold.

2
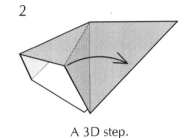
A 3D step.

3
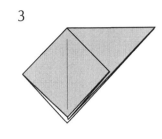

Petal Fold.

In a petal fold, one point is folded up while two opposite sides meet each other.

1
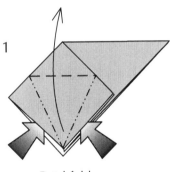
Petal-fold.

2
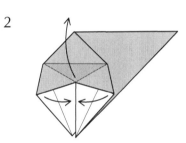
A 3D step.

3
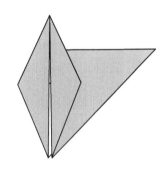

Inside Reverse Fold.

In an inside reverse fold, some paper is folded between layers. Here are two examples.

1
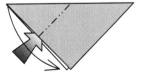
Reverse-fold.

2

1
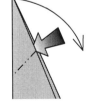
Reverse-fold.

2

Preliminary Fold.

The Preliminary Fold is the starting point for many models. The maneuver in step 3 occurs in many other models.

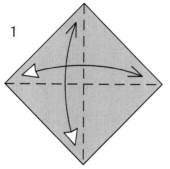

1

Fold and unfold.

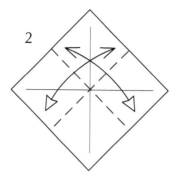

2

Fold and unfold.

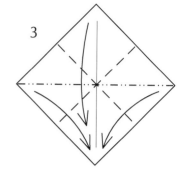

3

Collapse the square by bringing the four corners together.

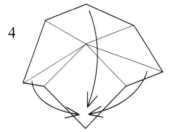

4

This is 3D.

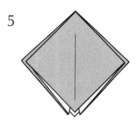

5

Preliminary Fold

Bird Base.

Historically, the Bird Base has been a very popular starting point. The folds used in it occur in many models.

1

Begin with the Preliminary Fold. Kite-fold, repeat behind.

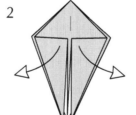

2

Unfold, repeat behind.

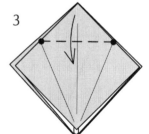

3

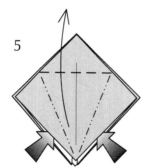

4

Unfold.

5

Petal-fold, repeat behind.

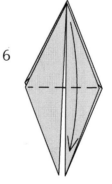

6

Repeat behind.

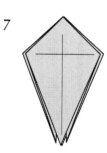

7

Bird Base

Objects

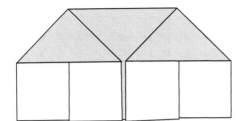

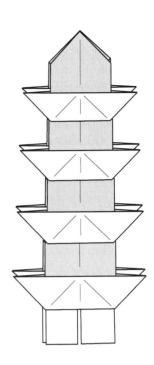

With a large collection of models including a house, pagoda, stars, table, waterbomb and more, you can create scenes and fold classic favorites. The models in this section are traditional designs. Several use the blintz fold, where the corners meet in the center. The waterbomb base is also used for several models.

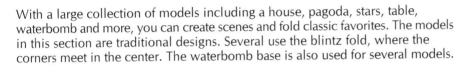

Cup

1

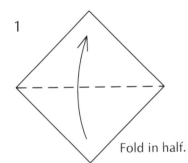

Fold in half.

2

Fold the top layer down.

3

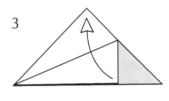

Unfold.

4

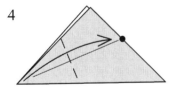

Fold the corner to the dot.

5

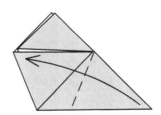

Fold the other corner.

6

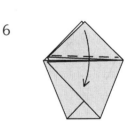

Fold the top layer down.

7

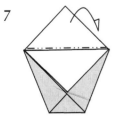

Fold behind along the mountain fold line.

8

Place your finger inside to open the cup.

9

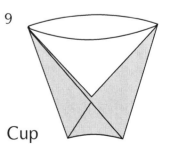

Cup

Wallet

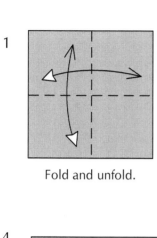

1 Fold and unfold.

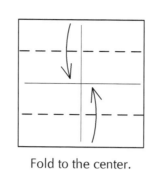

2 Fold to the center.

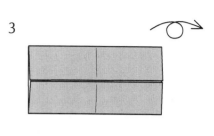

3

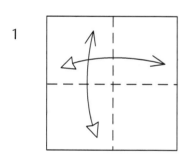

4 Fold to the center.

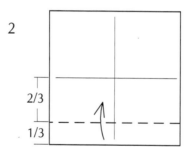

5 Fold in half.

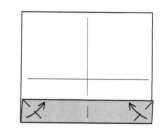

6 Wallet

Envelope

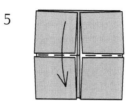

1 Fold and unfold.

2 Fold up one-third.

3

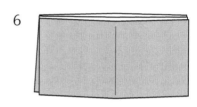

4

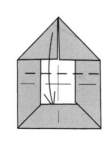

5 Fold to the center.

6 Tuck inside.

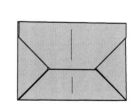

7 Envelope

Pin Wheel

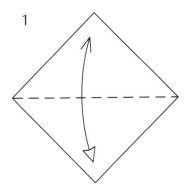

1

Fold and unfold.

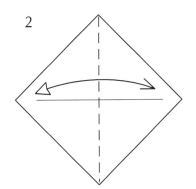

2

Fold and unfold.

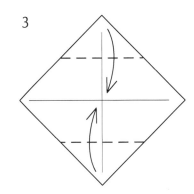

3

Fold two opposite
corners to the center.

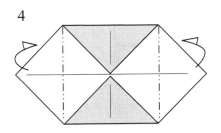

4

Fold the corners behind.

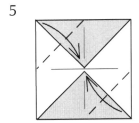

5

Fold two corners
to the center.

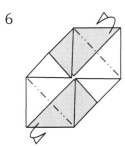

6

Fold the corners
behind.

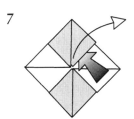

7

Place your finger inside
to pull out the corner.

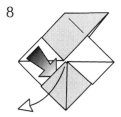

8

Pull out the
lower corner.

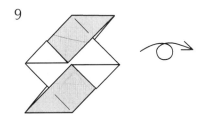

9

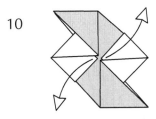

10

Pull out the
white corners.

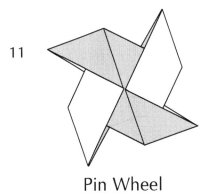

11

Pin Wheel

House

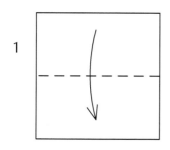

1

Fold in half.

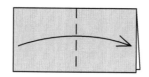

2

Fold in half.

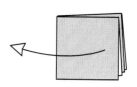

3

Unfold.

4

Fold to the center.

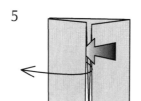

5

Place your finger inside for this squash fold.

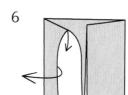

6

Continue opening the model, pushing down on the top.

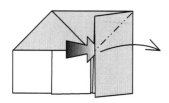

7

Squash-fold.

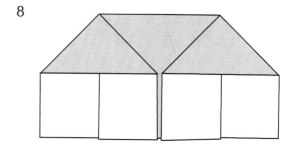

8

House

Piano

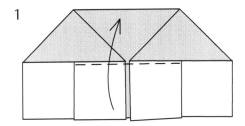

1

Begin with the house. Lift up.

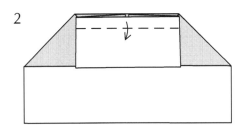

2

Fold a thin strip.

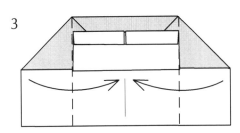

3

Fold to the center.

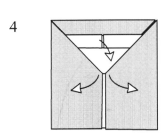

4

Open.

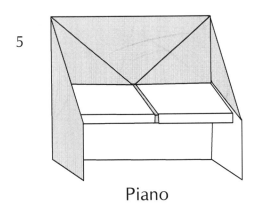

5

Piano

Fortune Teller

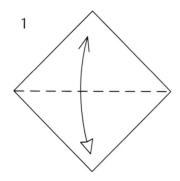

1

Fold and unfold.

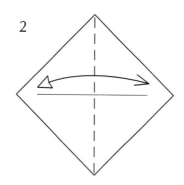

2

Fold and unfold.

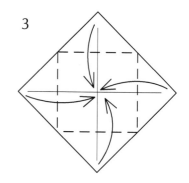

3

Fold the corners
to the center.

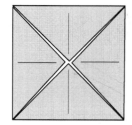

4

This is the Blintz Fold.

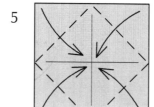

5

Fold to the center.

6

Fold in half.

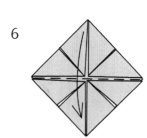

7

Squash-fold.

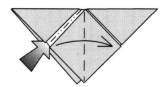

8

9

Squash-fold.

10

Spread the
four corners.

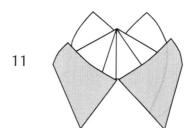

11

Fortune Teller
(or Cootie Catcher)

In England this is often used
as a salt cellar, and in Japan
as a candy dish.

Lantern

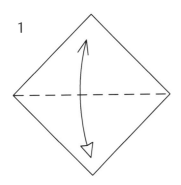

1 Fold and unfold.

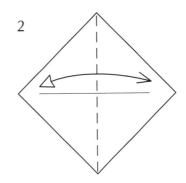

2 Fold and unfold.

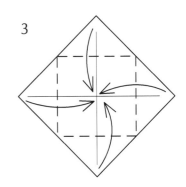

3 Fold the corners to the center.

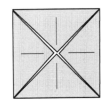

4 This is the Blintz Fold. Turn over and rotate.

  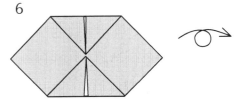

5 Fold the top and bottom to the center.

6

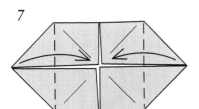  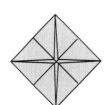

7 Fold to the center.

8 Fold the corners to the center.

9

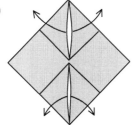

10 Open the top and bottom.

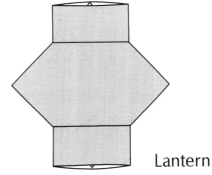

11 Lantern

Green Tea Cup

1

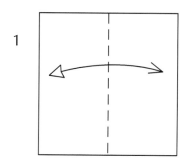

Fold and unfold.

2

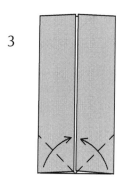

Fold to the center.

3

Fold to the center.

4

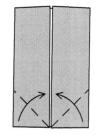

Fold behind.

5

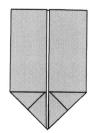

Fold to the center.

6

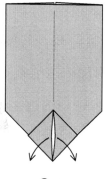

7

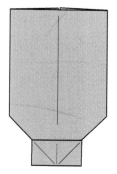

Open.

8

Green Tea Cup

Table

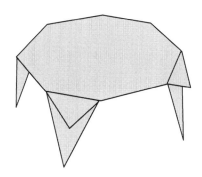

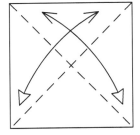

1

Fold and unfold.

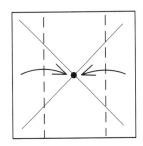

2

Fold to the center.

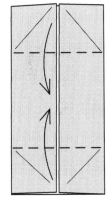

3

Fold to the center.

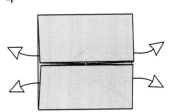

4

Pull out the corners.

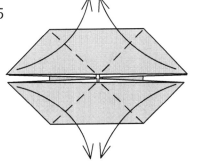

5

Fold two flaps up
and two flaps down.

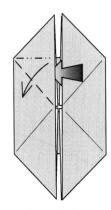

6

Squash-fold.

Table 21

7

Make three more
squash folds.

8

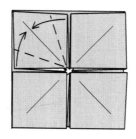

Fold to the center.

9

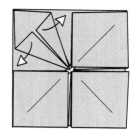

Unfold.

10

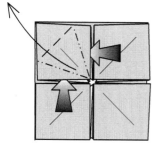

Petal-fold.

11

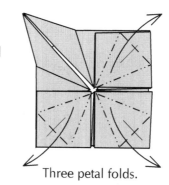

Three petal folds.

12

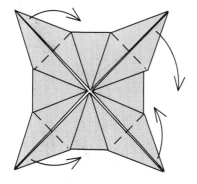

Fold the legs
straight up.

13

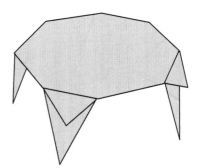

Table

Chair

1

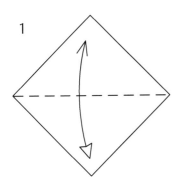

Fold and unfold.

2

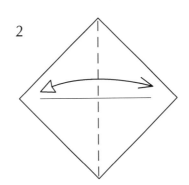

Fold and unfold.

3

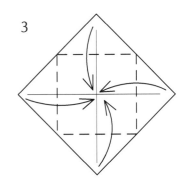

Fold the corners
to the center.

4

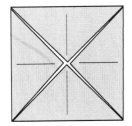

This is the Blintz Fold.

5

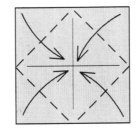

Fold to the center.

6

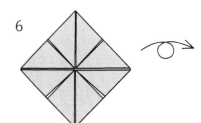

7

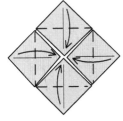

Fold to the center.

8

Turn over and rotate.

9

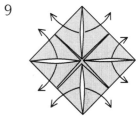

Open on four sides.

10

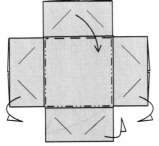

Fold one side to the
front and three behind.
The chair is 3D.

11

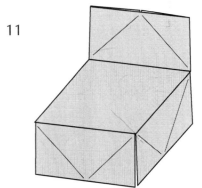

Chair

Fancy Card

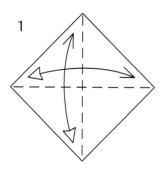

1

Fold and unfold.

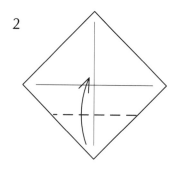

2

Fold above the center.

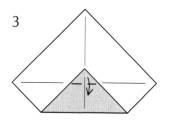

3

Fold along the
hidden crease.

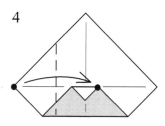

4

The dots will meet.

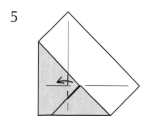

5

Fold along the
hidden crease.

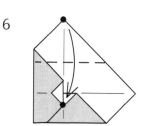

6

The dots will meet.

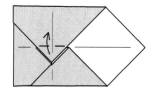

7

Fold along the
hidden crease.

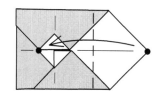

8

The dots will meet.

9

Fold along the
hidden crease.

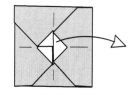

10

Unfold.

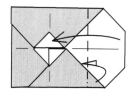

11

Reverse-fold.

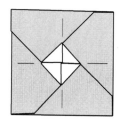

12

Fancy Card

Four-Pointed Star

1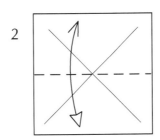

Fold and unfold.

2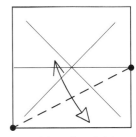

Fold and unfold.

3

Fold and unfold.

4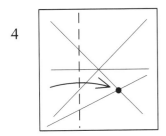

Fold to the dot.

5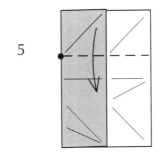

6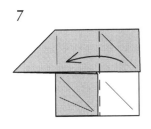

Pull out the corner.

7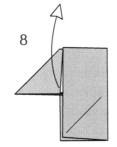

8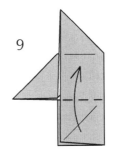

Pull out the corner.

9

10

Pull out the corner.

11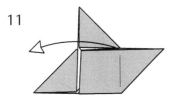

Pull out the corner.

12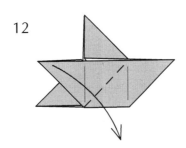

13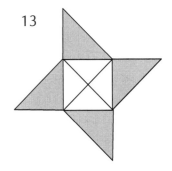

Four-Pointed Star

Five-Pointed Star

1

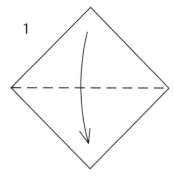

Fold in half.

2

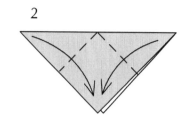

3

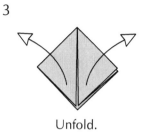

Unfold.

4

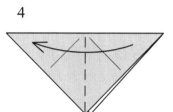

Fold in half.

5

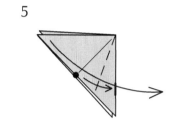

Fold the dot to
the bold line.

6

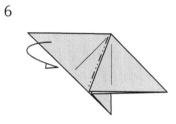

Fold behind.

7

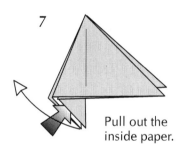

Pull out the
inside paper.

8

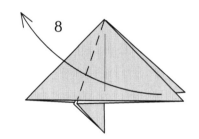

9

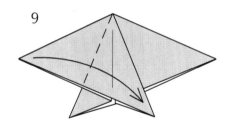

10

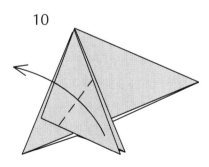

There are no guide
lines for this fold.

11

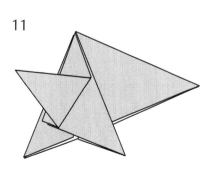

Repeat steps 9
and 10 behind.

12

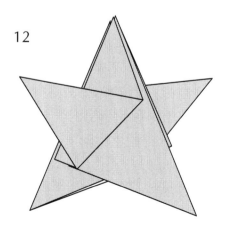

Five-Pointed Star

Six-Pointed Star

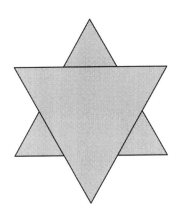

1

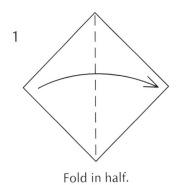

Fold in half.

2

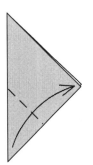

3

Unfold.

4

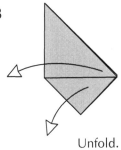

Bring the dots to the creases.

5

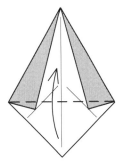

6

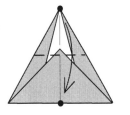

7

8

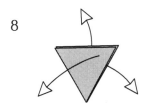

9

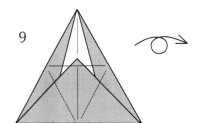

10

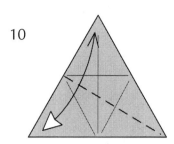

Fold in half and unfold.

11

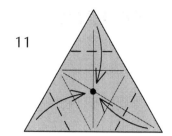

Fold to the center.

12

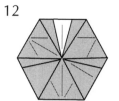

13

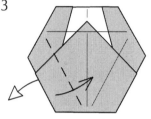

Fold along the crease and swing out from behind.

14

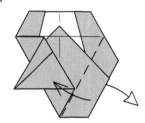

Fold along the crease and swing out from behind.

15

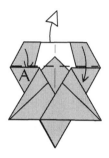

Tuck under A and swing out from behind.

16

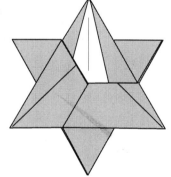

17

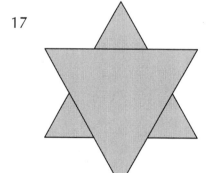

Six-Pointed Star

Waterbomb

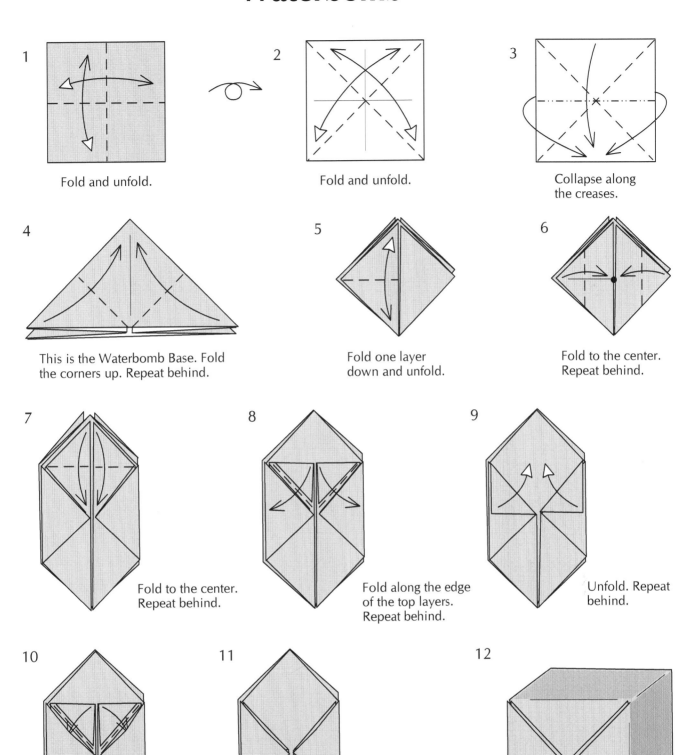

1 Fold and unfold.

2 Fold and unfold.

3 Collapse along the creases.

4 This is the Waterbomb Base. Fold the corners up. Repeat behind.

5 Fold one layer down and unfold.

6 Fold to the center. Repeat behind.

7 Fold to the center. Repeat behind.

8 Fold along the edge of the top layers. Repeat behind.

9 Unfold. Repeat behind.

10 Tuck inside the pockets. Repeat behind.

11 Holding the model like a star, with your fingers between the layers, blow into the bottom.

12 Waterbomb

Tent

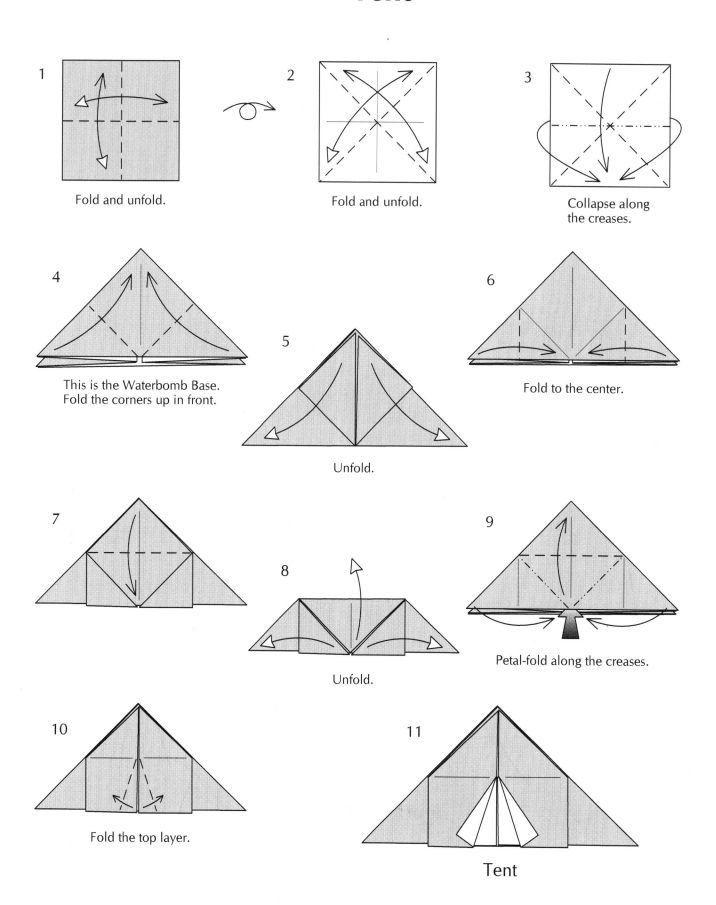

1 Fold and unfold.

2 Fold and unfold.

3 Collapse along the creases.

4 This is the Waterbomb Base. Fold the corners up in front.

5 Unfold.

6 Fold to the center.

7

8 Unfold.

9 Petal-fold along the creases.

10 Fold the top layer.

11 Tent

Church

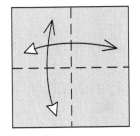

1

Fold and unfold.

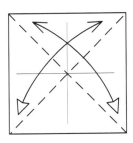

2

Fold and unfold.

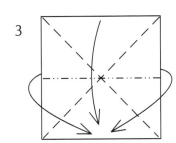

3

Collapse along
the creases.

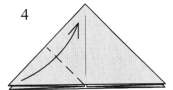

4

This is the Waterbomb
Base. Fold the flap up.

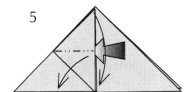

5

Squash-fold.

6

Repeat steps 4–5
on the right.

7

Repeat steps
4–6 behind.

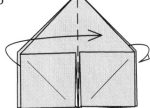

8

Fold to the right and
repeat behind. This is a
minor miracle.

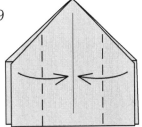

9

Fold the top layers to the
center. Repeat behind.

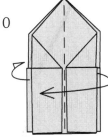

10

Minor miracle.

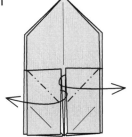

11

Squash folds.

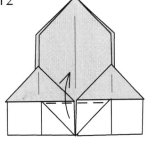

12

Fold up.

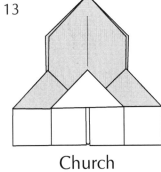

13

Church

Pagoda

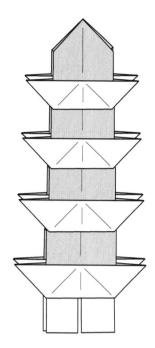

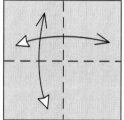

1 Fold and unfold.

 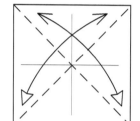

2 Fold and unfold.

3 Collapse along the creases.

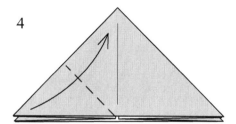

4 This is the Waterbomb Base. Fold the flap up.

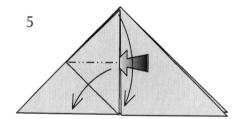

5 Squash-fold.

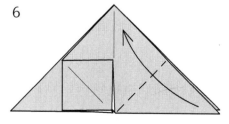

6 Repeat steps 4–5 on the right.

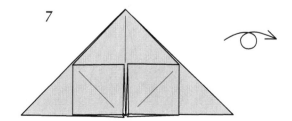

7

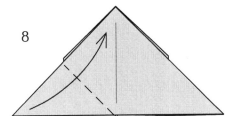

8

Repeat steps 4–6.

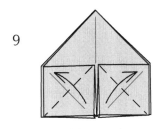

9

Fold up and
repeat behind.

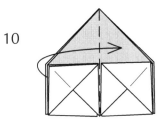

10

Fold to the right
and repeat behind.

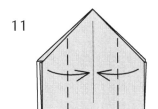

11

Fold the top layers to the
center. Repeat behind.

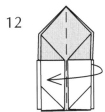

12

Fold to the left and
repeat behind.

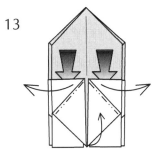

13

Spread the paper.
Repeat behind.

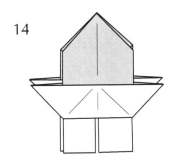

14

This is one unit. Fold
several in decreasing
sizes and stack them.

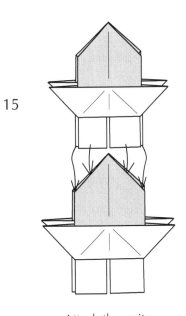

15

Attach the units.

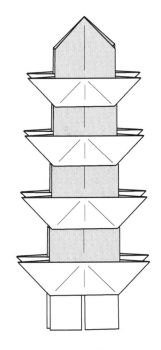

16

Pagoda

Lover's Knot

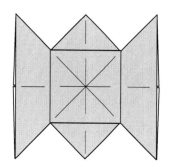

1

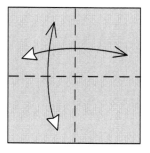

Fold and unfold.

2

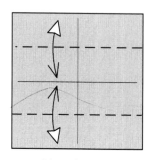

Fold to the center
and unfold.

3

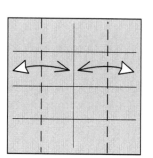

Fold to the center
and unfold.

4

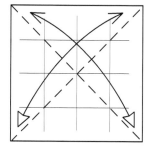

Fold and unfold.

5

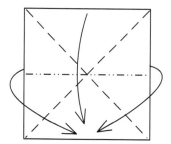

Collapse along
the creases.

6

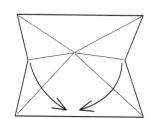

A 3D intermediate step.

7

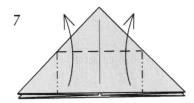

This is the Waterbomb Base.
Valley-fold along the crease.

8

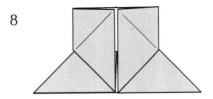

Repeat step 7 behind.

9

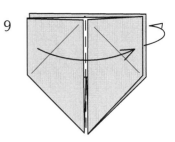

Fold to the right.
Repeat behind.

10

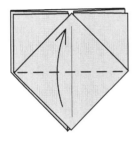

Fold up and
repeat behind.

11

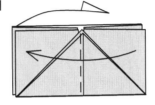

Fold to the left.
Repeat behind.

12

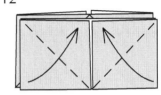

Fold up and
repeat behind.

13

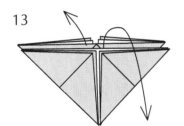

Spread, open, and
flatten. Rotate.

14

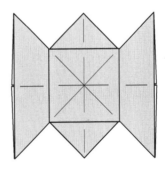

Lover's Knot

Hats

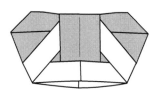 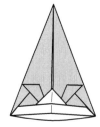 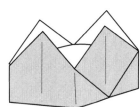

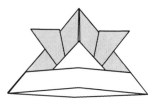

Hats are fun for all occasions, especially for children parties. Fold them large enough to wear. Here is a wide variety of mostly traditional models. The traditional turban and pirate hat are from rectangles so I designed variations from a square. The chef's hat is my design while the rest are traditional favorites. For the new folder, I would recommend starting with the easiest models. This includes the tall cap, pirate hat, and samurai hat.

Pirate Hat

Variation of
Traditional Hat by
John Montroll

1

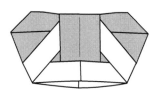

Fold in half.

2

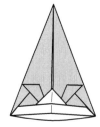

Fold the top layer down. The amount is not important.

3

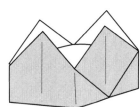

Fold behind.

4

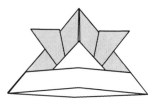

Unfold and rotate.

5

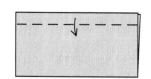

Fold in half.

6

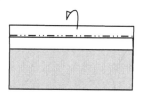

Fold to the center.

7

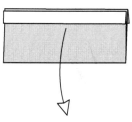

Repeat behind. Rotate the top to the bottom.

8

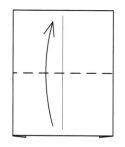

Open.

9

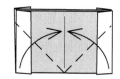

Pirate Hat

Tall Cap

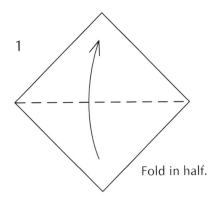

1

Fold in half.

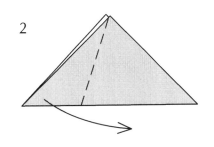

2

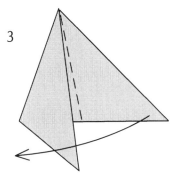

3

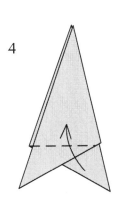

4

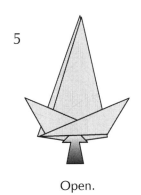

5

Open.

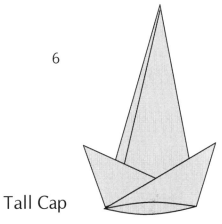

6

Tall Cap

Robin's Hat

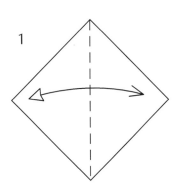

1

Fold and unfold.

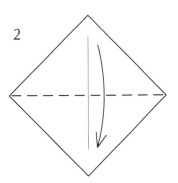

2

Fold down.

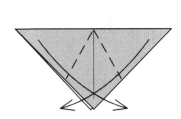

3

Trisect the angle.

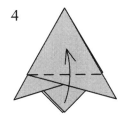

4

Fold everything up
but the bottom layer.

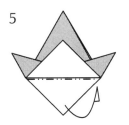

5

Fold behind.

6

Open.

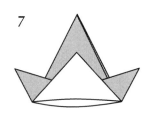

7

Robin's Hat

Samurai Hat

1

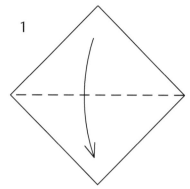

Fold in half.

2

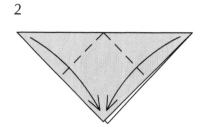

Fold the corners down
to meet at the bottom.

3

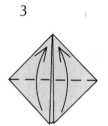

Fold the corners
to the top.

4

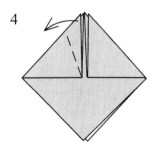

Fold a corner out.

5

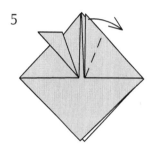

Repeat on the
other side.

6

7

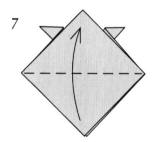

Fold the top layer up.

8

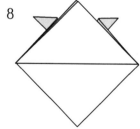

9

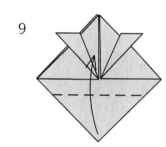

Fold up.

10

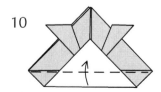

Fold a thin strip.

11

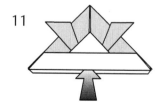

Place your finger
inside to open the hat.

12

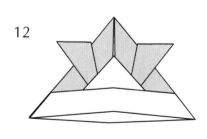

Samurai Hat

Party Hat

1

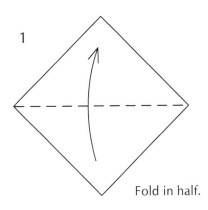

Fold in half.

2

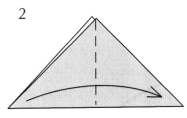

Fold in half.

3

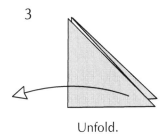

Unfold.

4

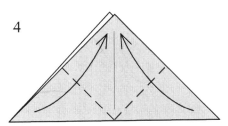

Fold the corners to the top.

5

Turn over and rotate
the dot to the bottom.

6

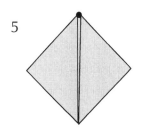

Kite-fold. Fold to the
center to form a kite.

7

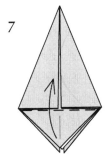

Fold one layer up.

8

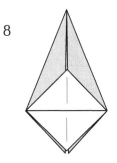

9

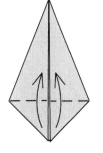

Fold the two
corners up.

10

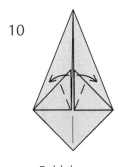

Fold the two
corners.

11

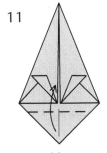

Fold up.

12

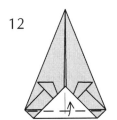

Fold a thin strip up.

13

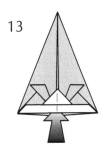

Open the hat.

14

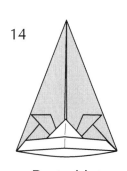

Party Hat

Cowboy Hat

1

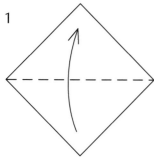

Fold in half.

2

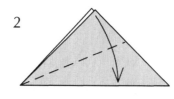

Fold the top layer down.

3

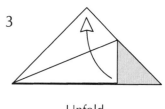

Unfold.

4

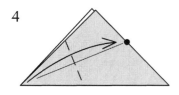

Fold the corner to the dot.

5

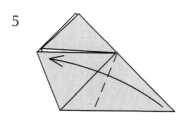

Fold the other corner.

6

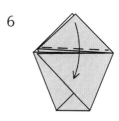

Fold the top layer down.

7

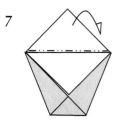

Fold behind along the mountain fold line. Rotate the top to the bottom.

8

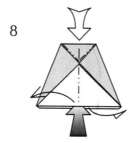

Place your finger inside to open at the bottom. Push in at the top. Make the model 3D, then flatten.

9

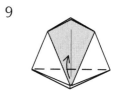

Fold up. Repeat behind.

10

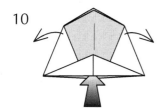

Spread on both sides and open the hat.

11

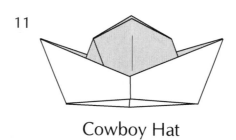

Cowboy Hat

Chef's Hat

Designed by John Montroll

1

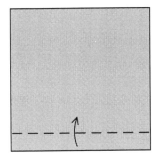

Fold a strip up.
The size can vary.

2

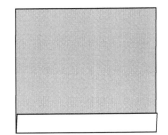

3

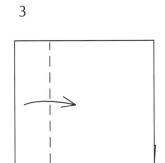

Fold to the right.
The size can vary.

4

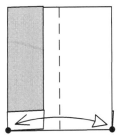

Fold and unfold.

5

Tuck inside.

6

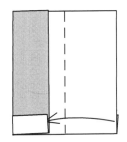

Fold and unfold.

7

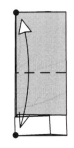

Tuck inside.

8

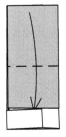

Open.

9

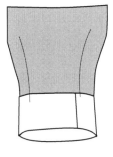

Chef's Hat

Officer's Hat

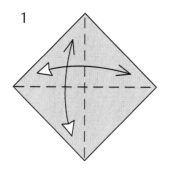

1

Fold and unfold.

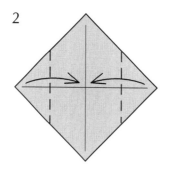

2

Fold two corners
to the center.

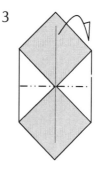

3

Fold behind.

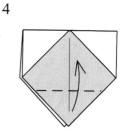

4

Fold up. The amount
is not important.
Repeat behind.

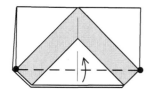

5

Fold up. Repeat behind.

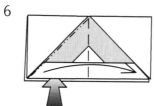

6

Squash-fold.

7

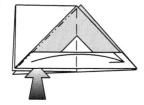

8

Squash-fold.

9

Fold the top layer
down. Repeat behind.

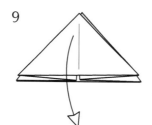

10

Fold to the center.
Repeat behind.

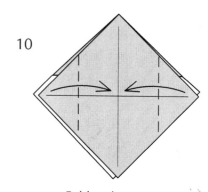

11

Fold up. Repeat
behind.

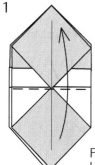

12

Open and
spread the hat.

13

Officer's Hat

Autumn Hat

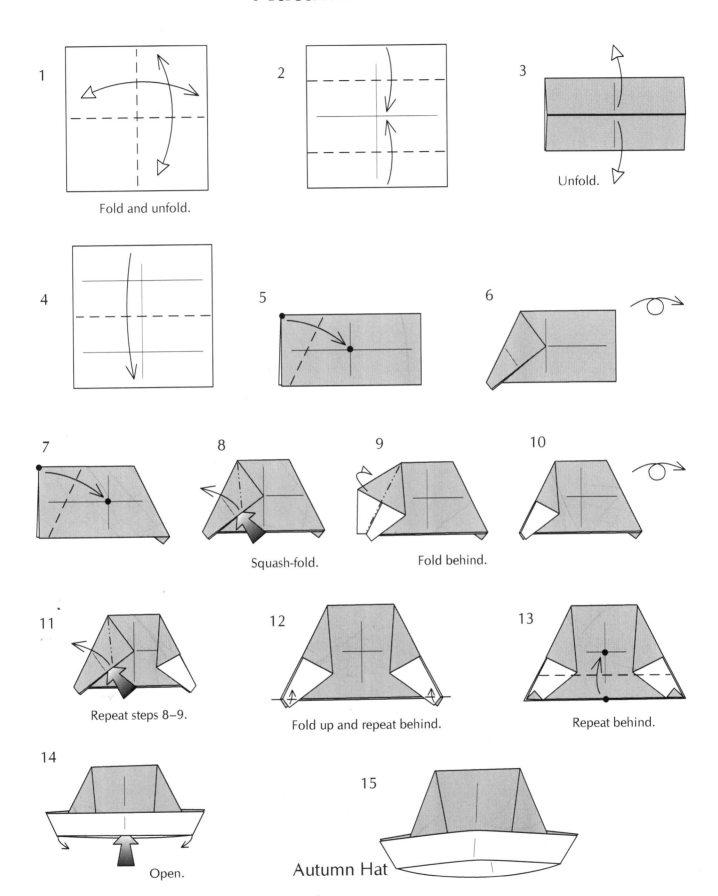

1 Fold and unfold.

2

3 Unfold.

4

5

6

7

8 Squash-fold.

9 Fold behind.

10

11 Repeat steps 8–9.

12 Fold up and repeat behind.

13 Repeat behind.

14 Open.

15 Autumn Hat

Navy Cap

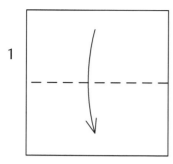

1 Fold in half.

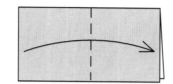

2 Fold in half.

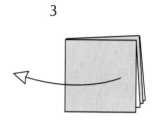

3 Unfold.

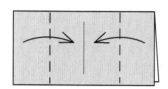

4 Fold to the center.

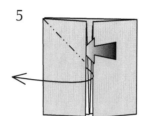

5 Squash-fold.

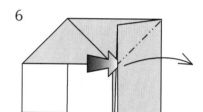

6 Squash-fold.

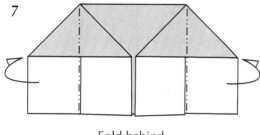

7 Fold behind.

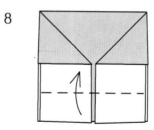

8 Fold up and repeat behind.

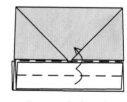

9 Repeat behind.

10 Push in at the top and open at the bottom.

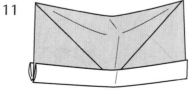

11 Navy Cap

Crown

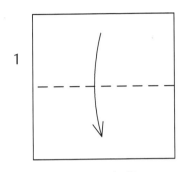

1

Fold in half.

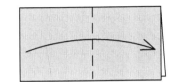

2

Fold in half.

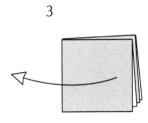

3

Unfold.

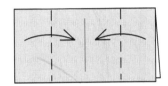

4

Fold to the center.

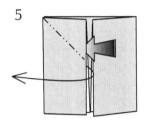

5

Squash-fold.

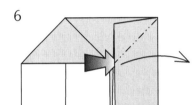

6

Squash-fold.

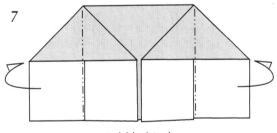

7

Fold behind.

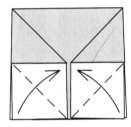

8

Repeat behind.

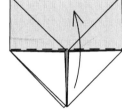

9

Repeat behind.

10

Push in at the top and
open at the bottom.

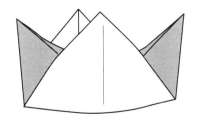

11

Crown

King's Crown

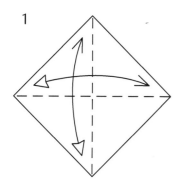

1

Fold and unfold.

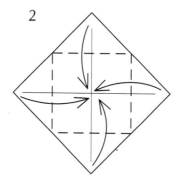

2

Fold the corners
to the center.

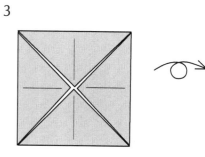

3

This is the Blintz Fold.

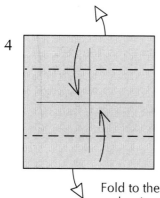

4

Fold to the center
and swing out
from behind.

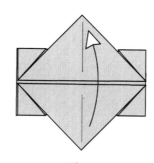

5

Lift up.

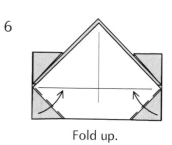

6

Fold up.

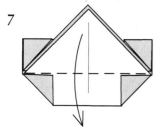

7

Fold along the crease.

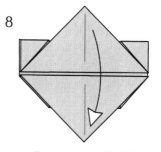

8

Repeat steps 5–7 in
the other direction.

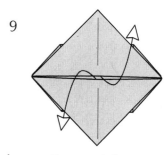

9

Open and shape
the crown.

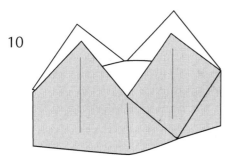

10

King's Crown

Helmet

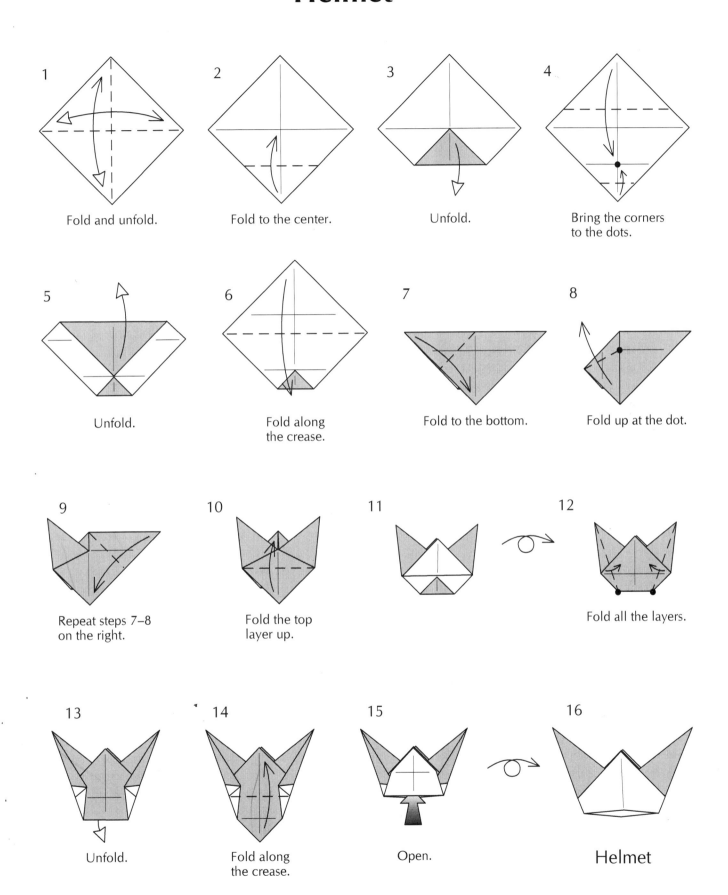

1 Fold and unfold.

2 Fold to the center.

3 Unfold.

4 Bring the corners to the dots.

5 Unfold.

6 Fold along the crease.

7 Fold to the bottom.

8 Fold up at the dot.

9 Repeat steps 7–8 on the right.

10 Fold the top layer up.

11

12 Fold all the layers.

13 Unfold.

14 Fold along the crease.

15 Open.

16 Helmet

Winged Hat

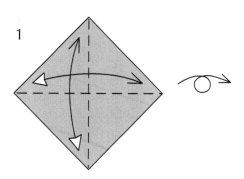

1

Fold and unfold.

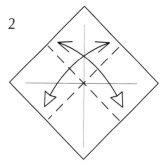

2

Fold and unfold.

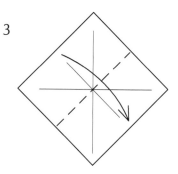

3

Fold in half and rotate.

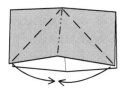

4

While holding in the air, use the crease lines to bring the lower corners together, then flatten.

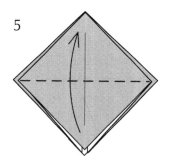

5

Fold the top layer up and repeat behind.

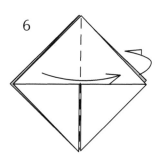

6

Fold to the right and repeat behind.

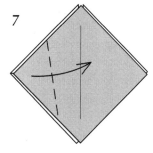

7

Repeat behind.

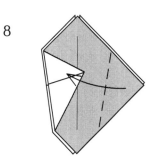

8

Repeat behind.

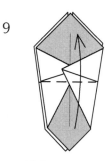

9

Fold the top layer up and repeat behind.

10

Tuck inside and repeat behind.

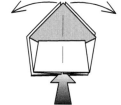

11

Open and spread.

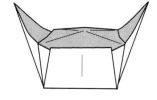

12

Winged Hat

Turban

Variantion of
Traditional Turban
by John Montroll

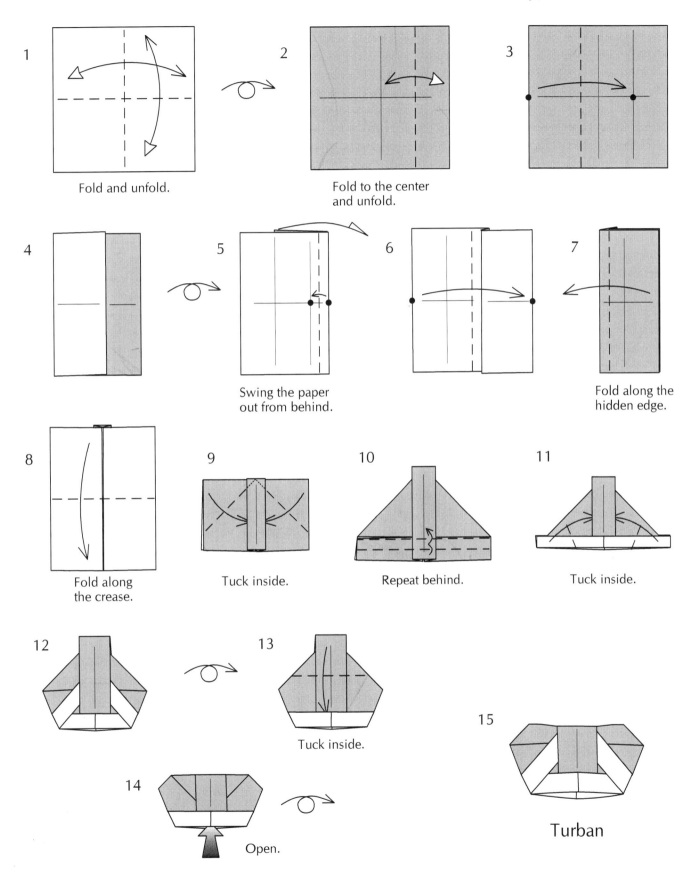

1. Fold and unfold.

2. Fold to the center and unfold.

3.

4.

5. Swing the paper out from behind.

6.

7. Fold along the hidden edge.

8. Fold along the crease.

9. Tuck inside.

10. Repeat behind.

11. Tuck inside.

12.

13. Tuck inside.

14. Open.

15.

Turban

Birds

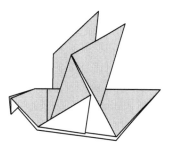

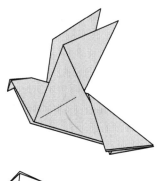

Birds make for beautiful origami subjects. These colorful creatures can be flying, wading, standing, or perching. Here is a collection of over a dozen traditional favorites including the flapping bird and crane.

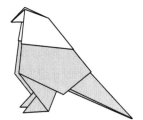

Wild Duck

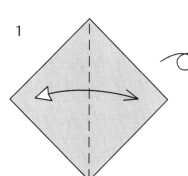

1

Fold and unfold.

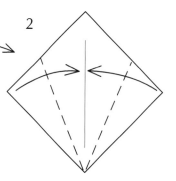

2

Kite-fold. Fold to the center to form a kite.

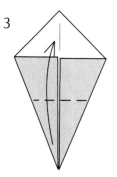

3

Fold up.

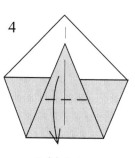

4

Fold down.

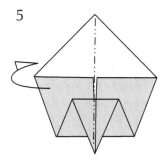

5

Fold in half and rotate.

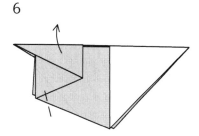

6

Slide the head up.

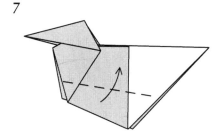

7

Fold up. Repeat behind.

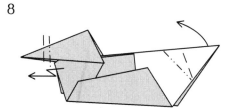

8

Fold in and out for the beak and tail.

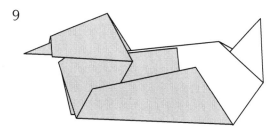

9

Wild Duck

Penguin

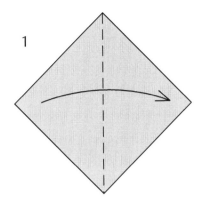

1

Fold in half.

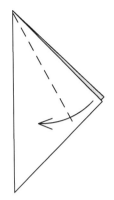

2

Fold the top layer.
Repeat behind.

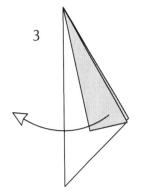

3

Unfold.

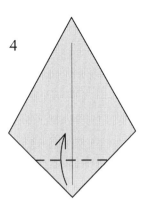

4

Fold up.

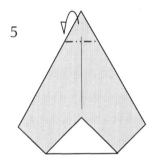

5

Fold behind.

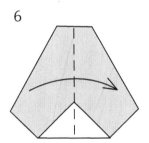

6

Fold in half.

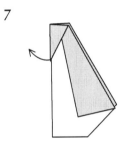

7

Slide up the head.

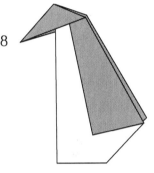

8

Penguin

Waterfowl

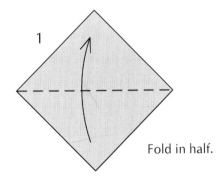

1

Fold in half.

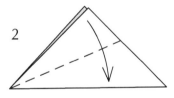

2

Fold to the bottom.
Repeat behind.

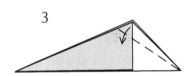

3

Repeat behind.

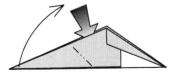

4

Place your finger
between the layers
for this reverse fold.

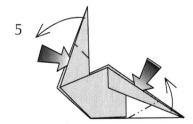

5

Reverse-fold the
head and tail.

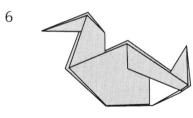

6

Waterfowl

Duck

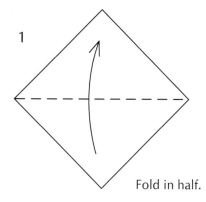

1

Fold in half.

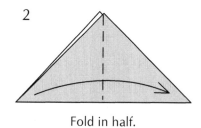

2

Fold in half.

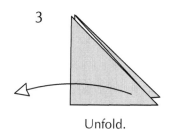

3

Unfold.

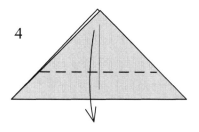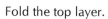

4

Fold the top layer.

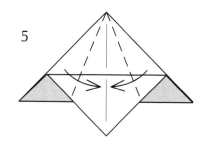

5

Fold to the center.

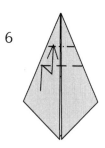

6

Fold back and forth.

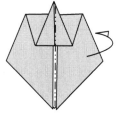

7

Fold behind and rotate.

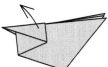

8

Lift up the neck
and head.

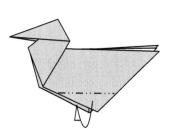

9

Fold inside and
repeat behind.

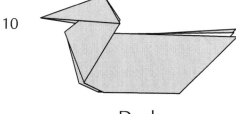

10

Duck

Swan

1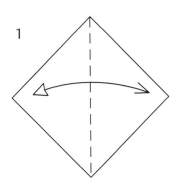

Fold and unfold.

2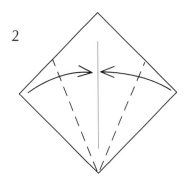

Kite-fold.

3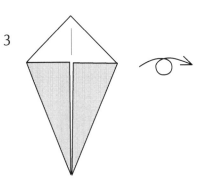

4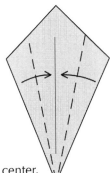

Fold to the center.

5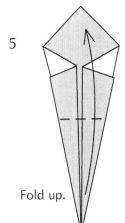

Fold up.

6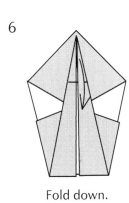

Fold down.

7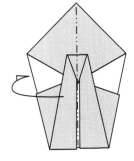

Fold behind.

8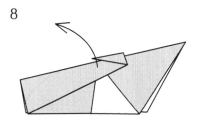

Slide the neck up.

9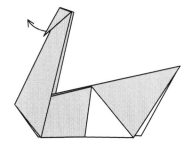

Slide the head up.

10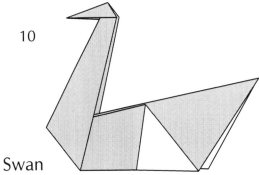

Swan

Flying Bird

1

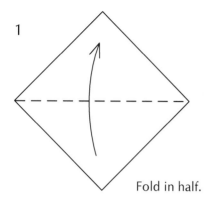

Fold in half.

2

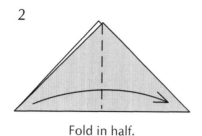

Fold in half.

3

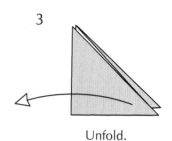

Unfold.

4

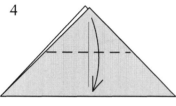

Fold both layers down.

5

Fold to the center.

6

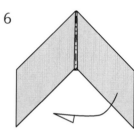

Fold in half and rotate.

7

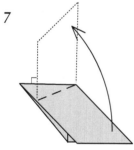

Fold the wing up to the dotted lines. Note the right angle. Repeat behind.

8

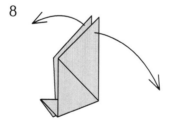

Spread the wings.

9

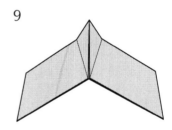

Flying Bird

10

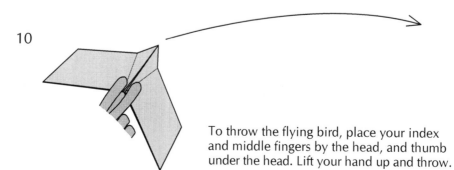

To throw the flying bird, place your index and middle fingers by the head, and thumb under the head. Lift your hand up and throw.

Pigeon

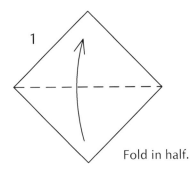

1

Fold in half.

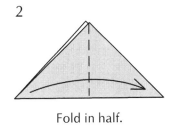

2

Fold in half.

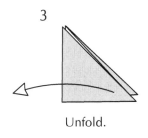

3

Unfold.

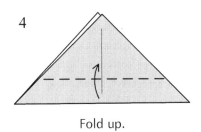

4

Fold up.

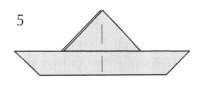

5

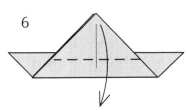

6

Fold one layer down.

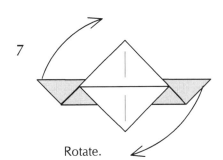

7

Rotate.

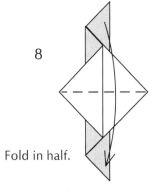

8

Fold in half.

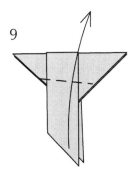

9

Fold the wing up,
repeat behind.

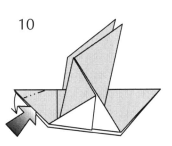

10

Reverse-fold the beak.

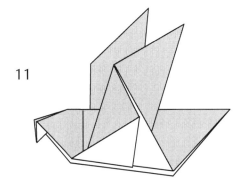

11

Pigeon

Dove

1

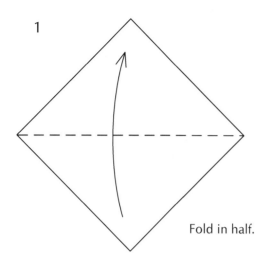

Fold in half.

2

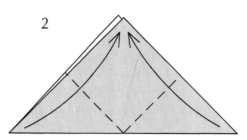

Fold the corners
up. Rotate 90°.

3

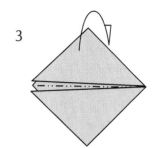

Fold behind.

4

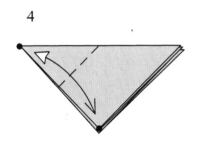

Fold all the layers and unfold.

5

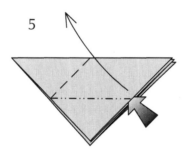

Squash-fold.
Repeat behind.

6

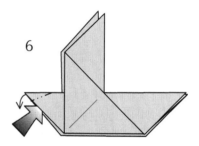

Reverse-fold the beak.

7

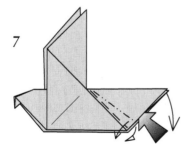

Place your finger
inside to bend the tail.

8

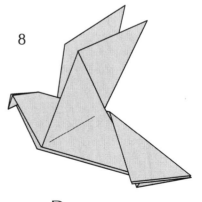

Dove

Pelican

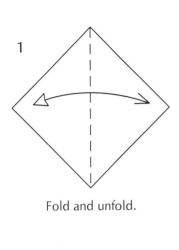

1

Fold and unfold.

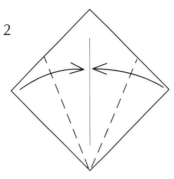

2

Kite-fold.

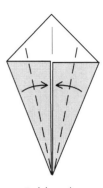

3

Fold to the center.

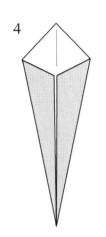

4

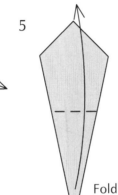

5

Fold the bottom tip above the top.

6

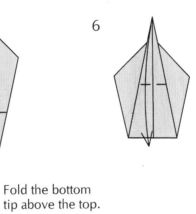

7

Fold in half and rotate.

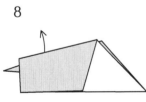

8

Slide out the neck and head.

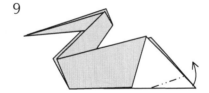

9

Fold the tail up.

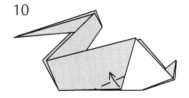

10

Repeat behind.

11

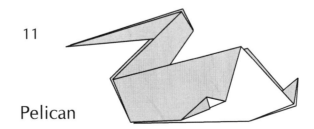

Pelican

Parakeet

1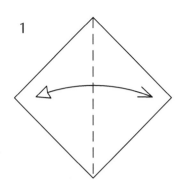

Fold and unfold.

2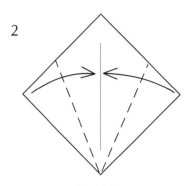

Kite-fold.

3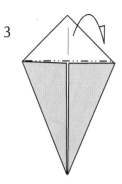

Fold behind.

4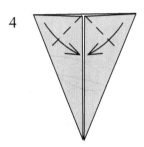

Fold to the center.

5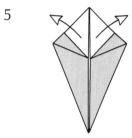

Unfold.

6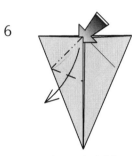

Squash-fold.

7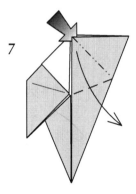

Squash-fold.

8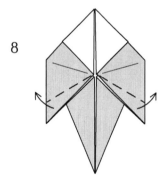

Fold up.

9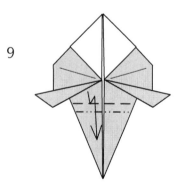

Fold back and forth.

10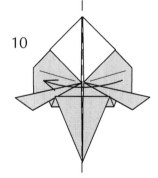

Fold in half and rotate.

11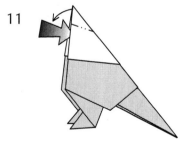

Reverse-fold the beak.

12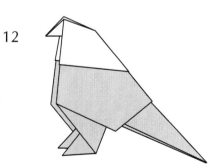

Parakeet

Pajarita

1

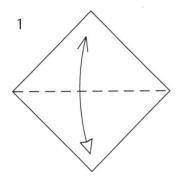

Foldand unfold.

2

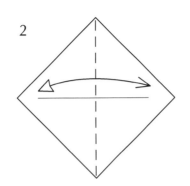

Fold and unfold.

3

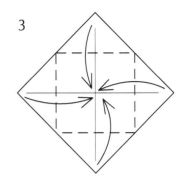

Fold the corners
to the center.

4

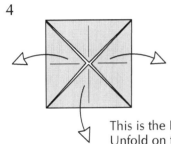

This is the Blintz Fold.
Unfold on three sides.

5

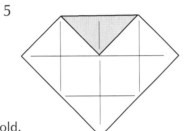

6

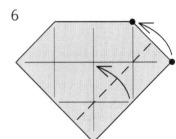

Fold to the dot.

7

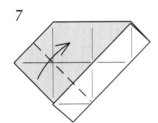

Fold on the left.

8

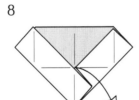

Pull out the corner.

9

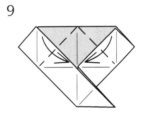

Fold to the center.

10

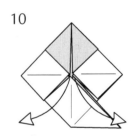

Pull out two corners.

11

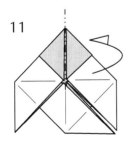

Fold in half.

12

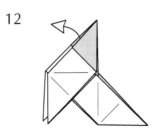

Pull out the corner.

13

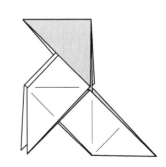

Pajarita
"Little Bird" in Spanish.

Flapping Bird

1

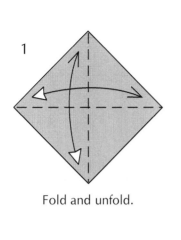

Fold and unfold.

2

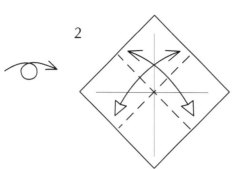

Fold and unfold.

3

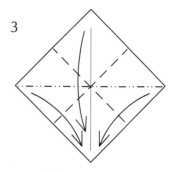

Fold along the creases.

4

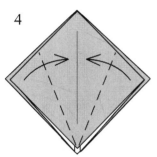

Kite-fold the top layers
and repeat behind.

5

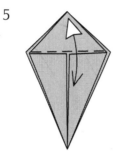

Fold all the layers
and unfold.

6

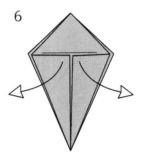

Unfold, repeat
behind.

7

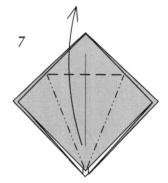

Petal-fold.

8

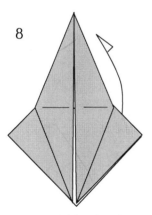

Petal-fold behind.

9

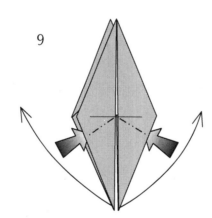

Make reverse folds.

10

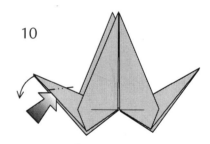

Reverse-fold.

11

Fold the wing out.
Repeat behind.

12

Pull the tail back and forth
while holding at the bottom
of the neck to flap the
wings. The white circles
show where to hold.

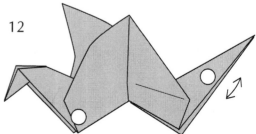

Flapping Bird

Crane

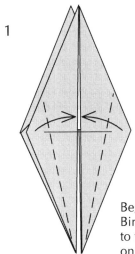

1

Begin with step 9 of the Flapping Bird. For this kite fold, fold close to the center line but not exactly on it. Repeat behind.

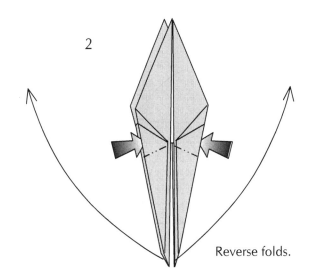

2

Reverse folds.

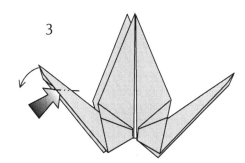

3

Reverse-fold.

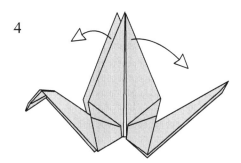

4

Pull the wings apart and let the body open.

5

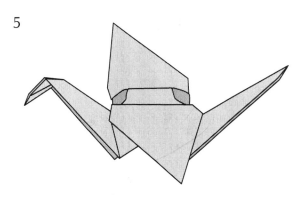

Crane

This is perhaps the most famous model in all of origami. The crane symbolizes peace and hope; a thousand cranes, often strung together, are folded for many occasions. Many Japanese children know this model. Being able to fold it is a milestone.

Boats

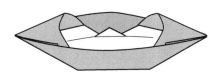
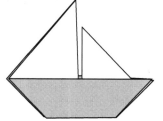
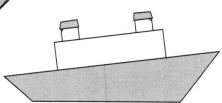

Origami boats are fun to make. Here is a collection of twelve simple boats, each folded from an uncut square. The traditional paper boat is from a rectangle so I designed a variation from a square. The ocean liner is my design while the rest are traditional favorites. For folding the row boat and Chinese fishing boat, one of the steps near the end is to wrap the paper inside-out to create a three-dimensional effect. The folding can be messy, so do it carefully.

——— Tall Sailboat ———

1

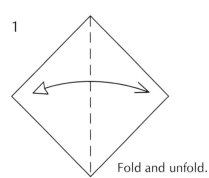

Fold and unfold.

2

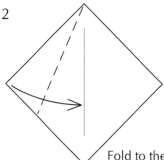

Fold to the center.

3

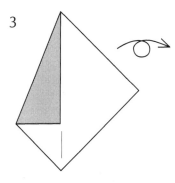

4

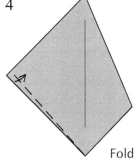

Fold a thin strip.

5

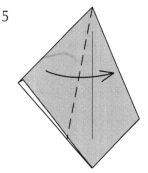

6

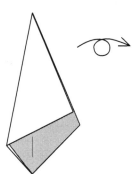

7

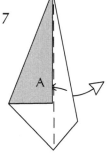

Fold under flap A and
swing out from behind.

8

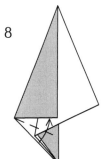

9

Fold behind.

10

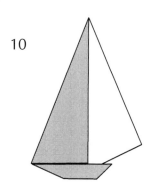

Tall Sailboat

Yacht

1

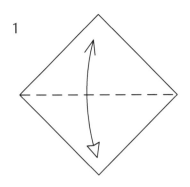

Fold and unfold.

2

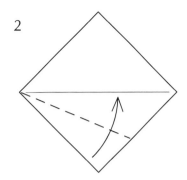

Fold to the center.

3

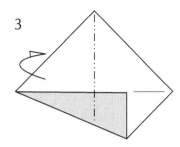

Fold in half and behind.

4

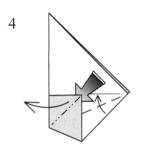

Squash-fold.

5

Fold all the layers behind.

6

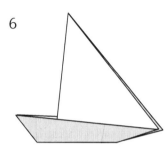

Yacht

Windsurfer

1

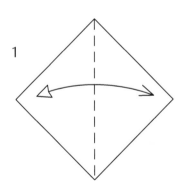

Fold and unfold.

2

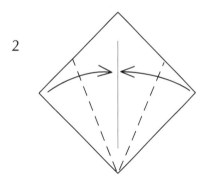

Kite-fold.

3

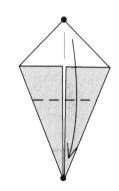

Fold in half.

4

Fold to the center.

5

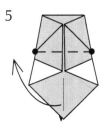

Fold straight up.

6

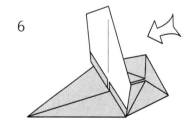

Blow to move
the windsurfer.

Windsurfer

Catamaran

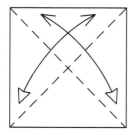

1 Fold and unfold.

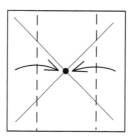

2 Fold to the center.

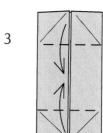

3 Fold to the center.

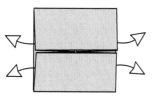

4 Pull out the corners.

5 Fold behind.

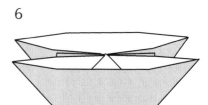

6 Catamaran

Sailboat

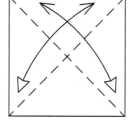

1 Fold and unfold.

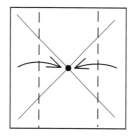

2 Fold to the center.

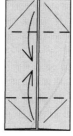

3 Fold to the center.

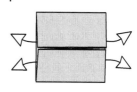

4 Pull out the corners.

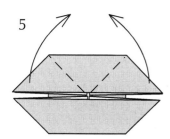

5 Fold up.

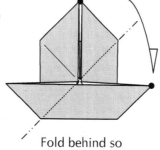

6 Fold behind so the dots meet.

7 Sailboat

Sailboat 2

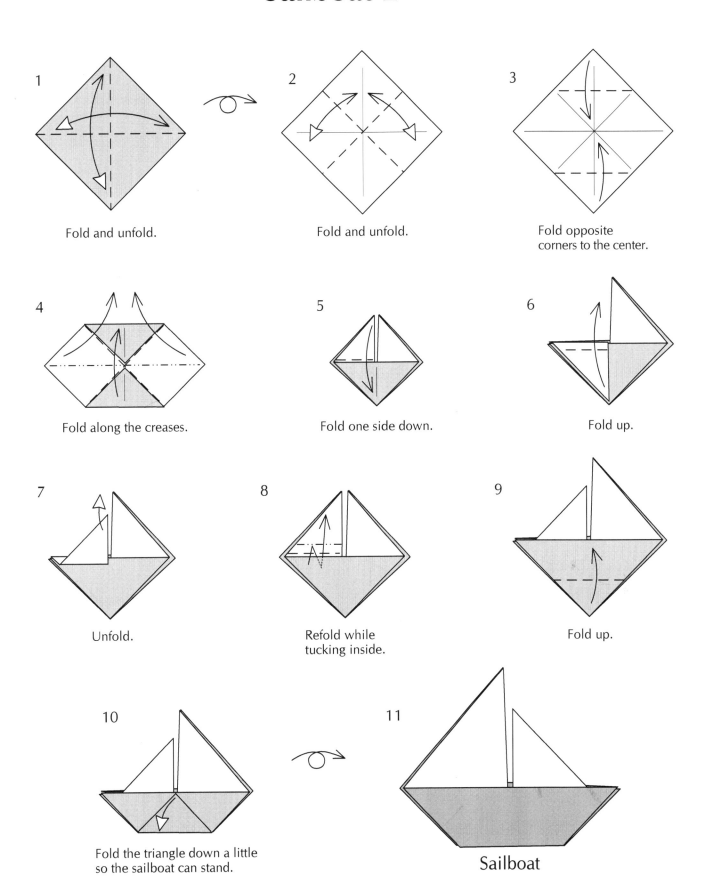

1 Fold and unfold.

2 Fold and unfold.

3 Fold opposite corners to the center.

4 Fold along the creases.

5 Fold one side down.

6 Fold up.

7 Unfold.

8 Refold while tucking inside.

9 Fold up.

10 Fold the triangle down a little so the sailboat can stand.

11 Sailboat

Boat

1

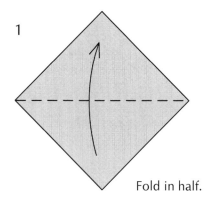

Fold in half.

2

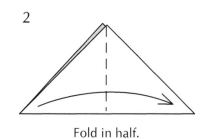

Fold in half.

3

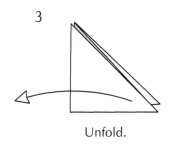

Unfold.

4

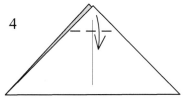

Fold the top layer down and repeat behind.

5

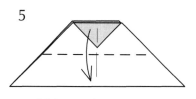

Fold the top layer to the bottom and repeat behind.

6

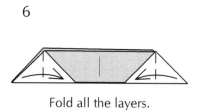

Fold all the layers.

7

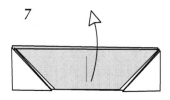

Unfold the top layer.

8

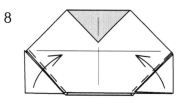

Fold the layers up.

9

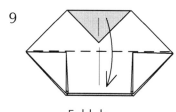

Fold down.

10

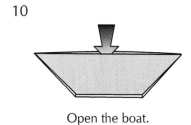

Open the boat.

11

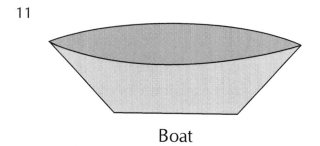

Boat

Paper Boat

This is a variation of the traditional boat from a rectangle.

1

Fold in half.

2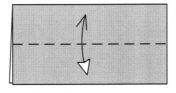

Fold the top layer in half and unfold.

3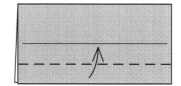

Fold the top layer to the crease. Repeat behind.

4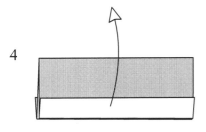

Unfold and rotate.

5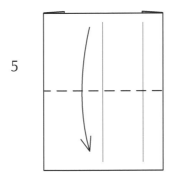

Fold in half.

6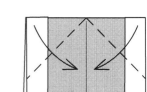

Fold to the center.

7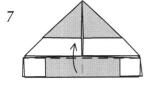

Fold the top layer up. Repeat behind.

8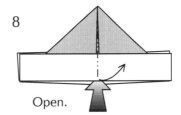

Open.

9

This is a 3D intermediate step. Continue and then flatten so the dots are on the left and right.

10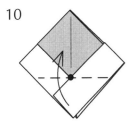

Fold up. Repeat behind.

11

Open. This is the same as steps 8 and 9.

12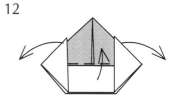

Fold up and spread on the left and right. Repeat behind.

13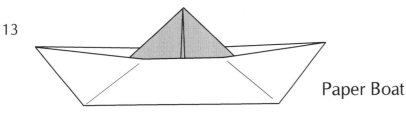

Paper Boat

Steamboat

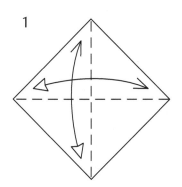

1

Fold and unfold.

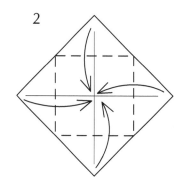

2

Fold the corners
to the center.

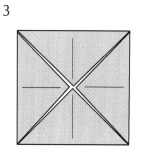

3

This is the Blintz Fold.

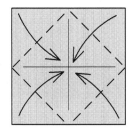

4

Fold to the center.

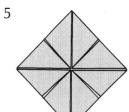

5

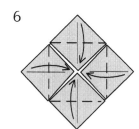

6

Fold to the center.

7

Turn over and rotate.

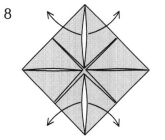

8

Open on two sides.

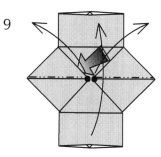

9

Fold in half and pop out the
two corners with the dots.

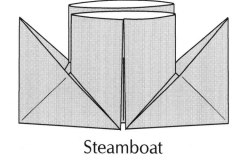

10

Steamboat

Row Boat

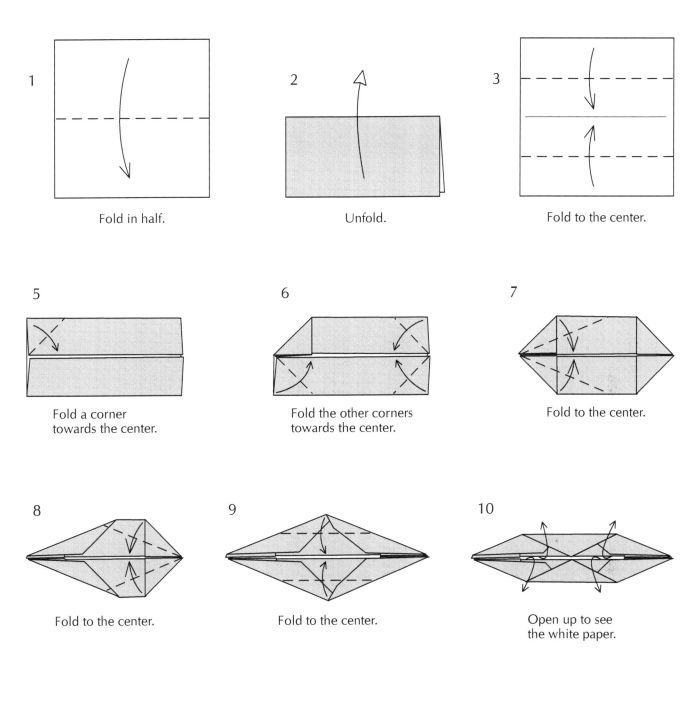

1 Fold in half.

2 Unfold.

3 Fold to the center.

5 Fold a corner towards the center.

6 Fold the other corners towards the center.

7 Fold to the center.

8 Fold to the center.

9 Fold to the center.

10 Open up to see the white paper.

11 Fold inside-out and turn over.

12

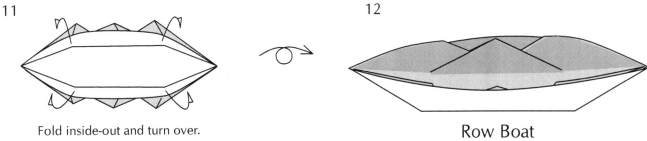

Row Boat

Chinese Fishing Boat

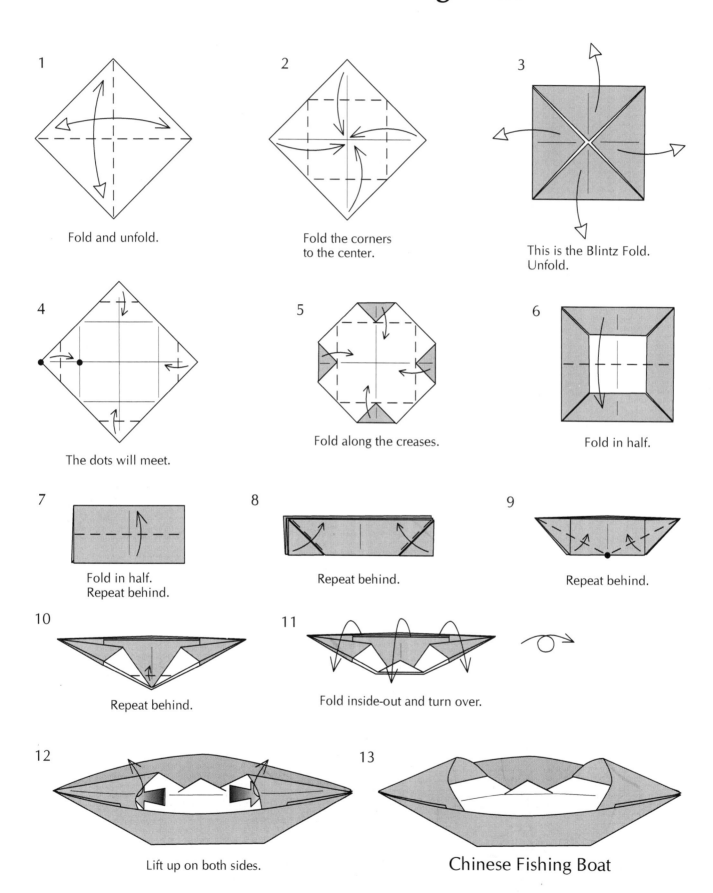

1
Fold and unfold.

2
Fold the corners
to the center.

3
This is the Blintz Fold.
Unfold.

4
The dots will meet.

5
Fold along the creases.

6
Fold in half.

7
Fold in half.
Repeat behind.

8
Repeat behind.

9
Repeat behind.

10
Repeat behind.

11
Fold inside-out and turn over.

12
Lift up on both sides.

13
Chinese Fishing Boat

Ocean Liner

Designed by John Montroll

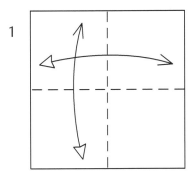

1 Fold and unfold.

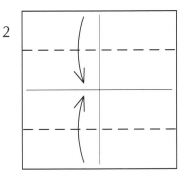

2 Fold to the center.

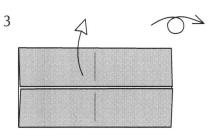

3 Unfold at the top.

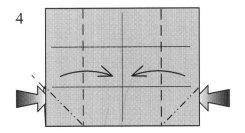

4 Squash folds.

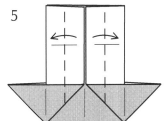

5

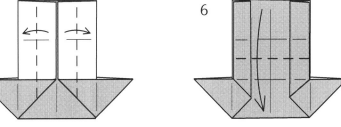

6 Fold in half.

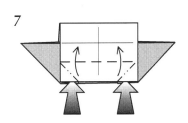

7 Squash folds.

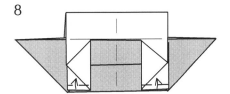

8 Fold thin strips.

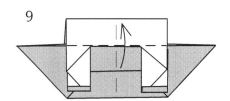

9 Fold up along the crease.

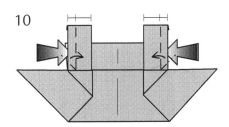

10 Make squash folds with a width of about 1/3.

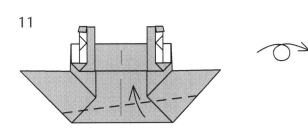

11

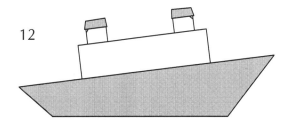

12

Ocean Liner

Fish

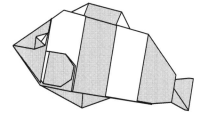
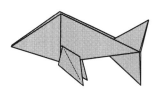
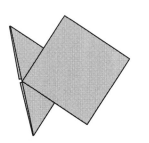
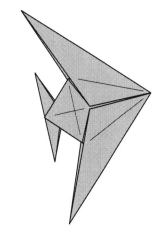

Fish are beautiful models to create with origami. You can make colorful aquarium scenes or "pictures" by drawing the sea background and pasting the folded fish. Here is a collection of simple sea creatures. Most are my designs and a few are traditional. For the new folder, I recommend starting with the easiest models which include the simple fish and carp.

Simple Fish

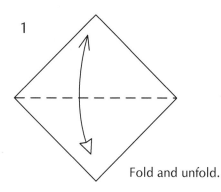

1

Fold and unfold.

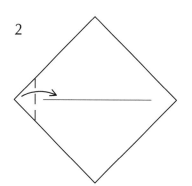

2

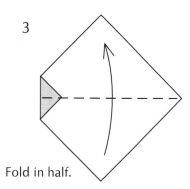

3

Fold in half.

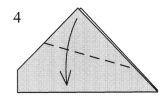

4

5

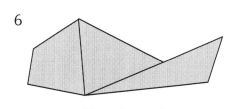

6

Simple Fish

Carp

1
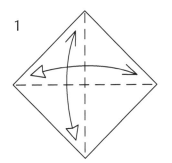
Fold and unfold.

2
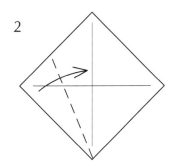
Fold to the center.

3
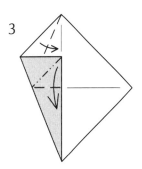
Squash-fold.

4
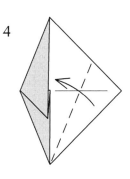
Repeat steps 2–3 on the right.

5
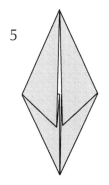

6
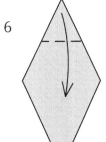
Fold down.

7
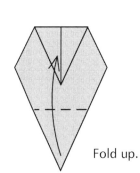
Fold up.

8
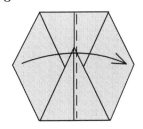
Fold in half.

9
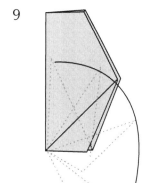
Slide out the point. Rotate.

10
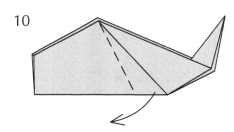
Fold the fin down, repeat behind.

11
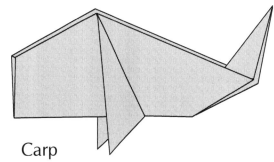
Carp

Big Fish

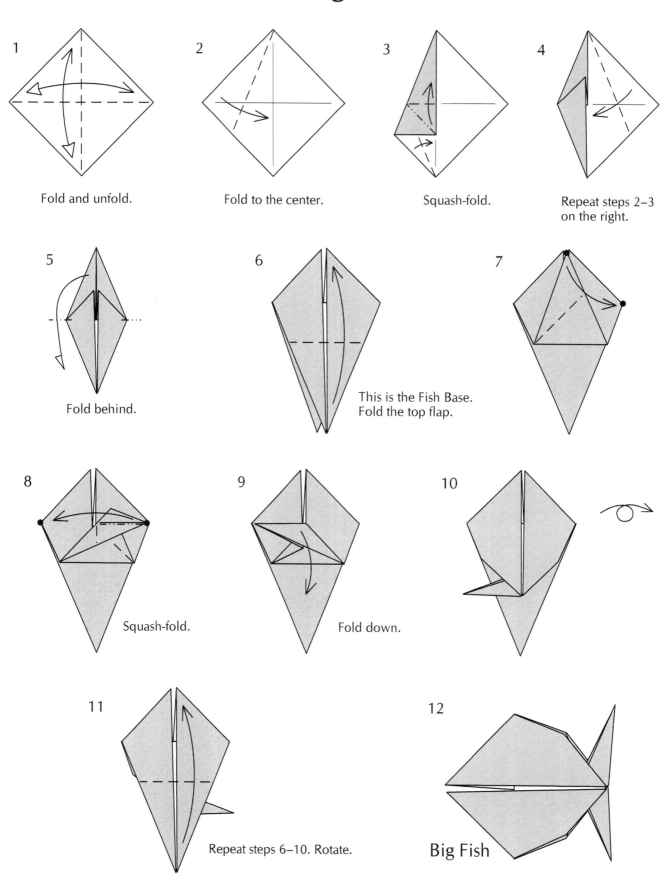

1   Fold and unfold.

2   Fold to the center.

3   Squash-fold.

4   Repeat steps 2–3 on the right.

5   Fold behind.

6   This is the Fish Base. Fold the top flap.

7

8   Squash-fold.

9   Fold down.

10

11   Repeat steps 6–10. Rotate.

12   Big Fish

Cute Fish

Designed by John Montroll

1

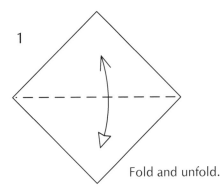

Fold and unfold.

2

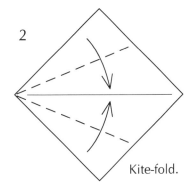

Kite-fold.

3

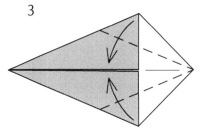

Fold to the center.

4

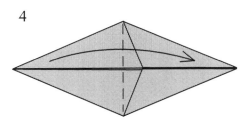

Fold in half.

5

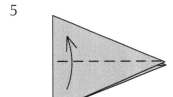

Fold in half.

6

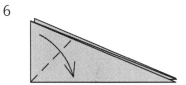

Repeat behind.

7

Unfold and repeat behind.

8

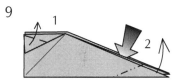

Repeat behind.

9

1. Fold the fin up and repeat behind.
2. Reverse-fold the tail.

10

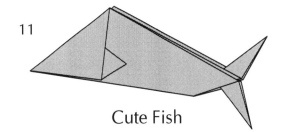

1. Repeat behind.
2. Reverse-fold the tail.

11

Cute Fish

Tropical Fish

Designed by John Montroll

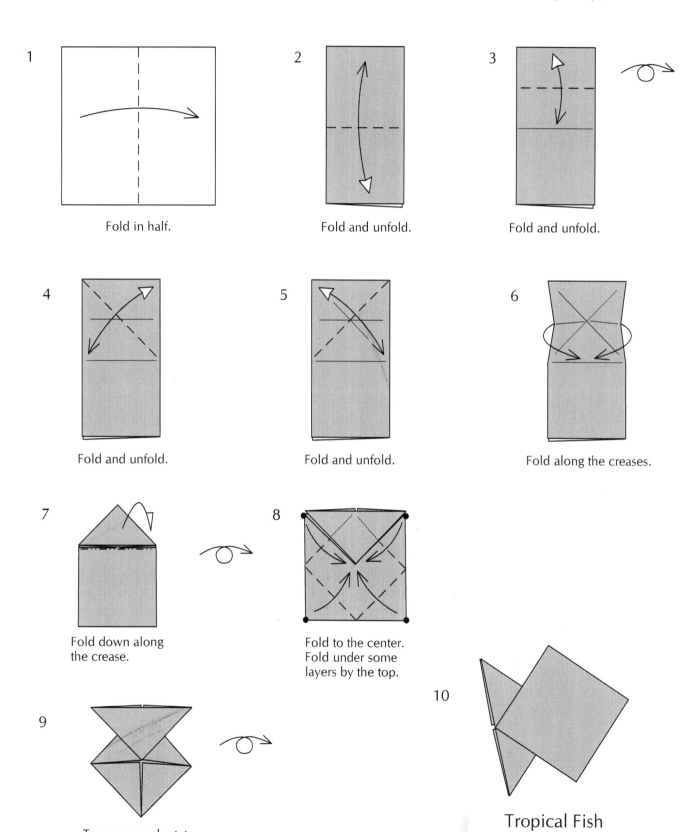

1 Fold in half.

2 Fold and unfold.

3 Fold and unfold.

4 Fold and unfold.

5 Fold and unfold.

6 Fold along the creases.

7 Fold down along the crease.

8 Fold to the center. Fold under some layers by the top.

9 Turn over and rotate.

10 Tropical Fish

Goldfish

Designed by John Montroll

1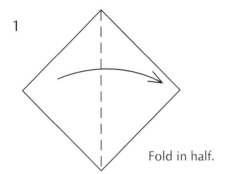

Fold in half.

2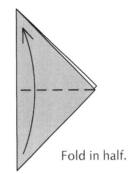

Fold in half.

3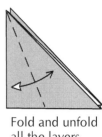

Fold and unfold
all the layers.

4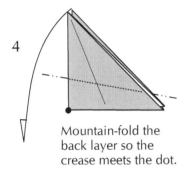

Mountain-fold the
back layer so the
crease meets the dot.

5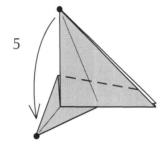

The dots will meet.

6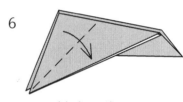

Fold along the crease.
Repeat behind.

7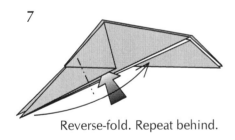

Reverse-fold. Repeat behind.

8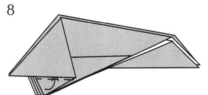

Tuck the top layer
inside. Repeat behind.

9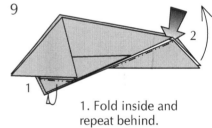

1. Fold inside and
repeat behind.
2. Reverse-fold.

10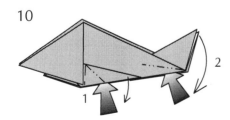

1. Squash-fold and
repeat behind.
2. Reverse-fold.

11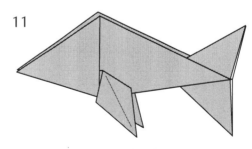

Goldfish

Angelfish

Designed by John Montroll

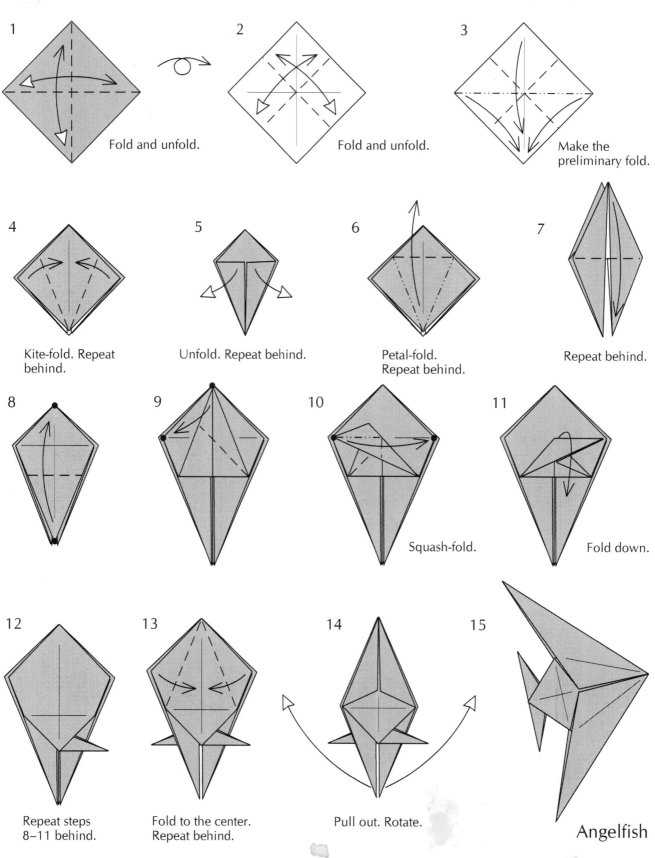

1
Fold and unfold.

2
Fold and unfold.

3
Make the preliminary fold.

4
Kite-fold. Repeat behind.

5
Unfold. Repeat behind.

6
Petal-fold. Repeat behind.

7
Repeat behind.

8

9

10
Squash-fold.

11
Fold down.

12
Repeat steps 8–11 behind.

13
Fold to the center. Repeat behind.

14
Pull out. Rotate.

15

Angelfish

Sea Horse

Designed by John Montroll

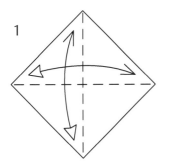

1

Fold and unfold.

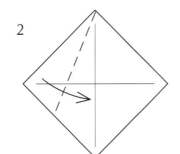

2

Fold to the center.

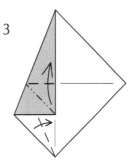

3

Squash-fold.

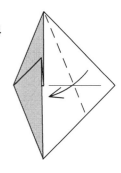

4

Repeat steps 2–3 on the right.

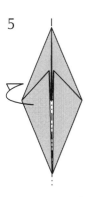

5

Fold behind.

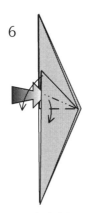

6

Squash-fold.
Repeat behind

7

Repeat behind.

8

Repeat behind.

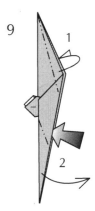

9

1. Fold at about an angle of one-third. Repeat behind.
2. Reverse-fold.

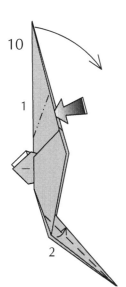

10

1. Reverse-fold.
2. Repeat behind.

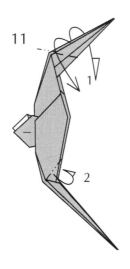

11

1. Outside-reverse-fold.
2. Repeat behind.

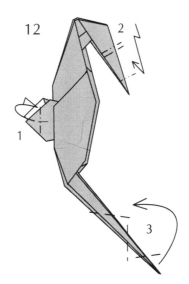

12

1. Repeat behind.
2. Shape the head with reverse folds.
3. Shape the tail with reverse folds.

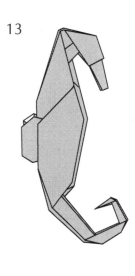

13

Sea Horse

Clown Fish

Designed by John Montroll

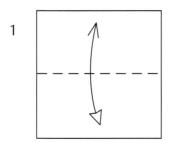

1 Fold and unfold.

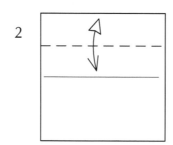

2 Fold to the center and unfold.

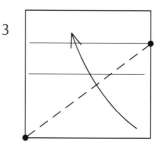

3 Fold up using the guides.

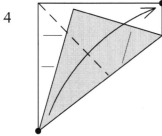

4 The dots will meet.

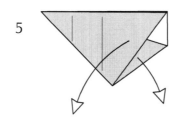

5 Unfold everything.

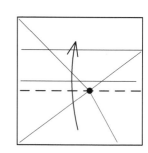

6 Fold up using the guides.

7

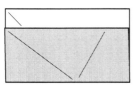

8 Fold in half.

9 Fold the top layer in half.

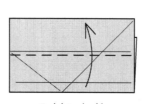

10 Unfold.

11 Bring the corners to the crease, folding both layers.

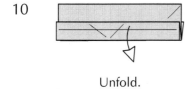

12 Fold up so the dots meet.

13

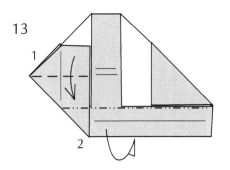

1. Fold down.
2. Fold behind.

14

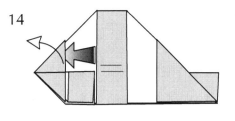

Pull out.

15

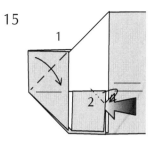

Part of the model is drawn.
1. Fold down.
2. Reverse-fold.

16

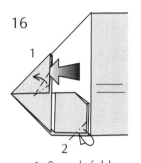

1. Squash-fold.
2. Fold behind.

17

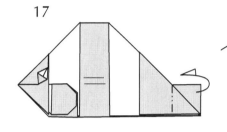

Fold behind.

18

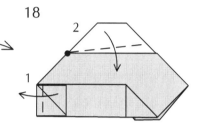

1. Fold to the left.
2. Fold down.

19

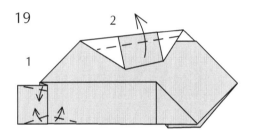

1. Shape the tail
   with small folds.
2. Fold up.

20

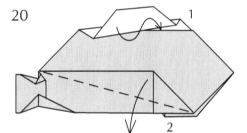

1. Tuck inside.
2. Fold down.

21

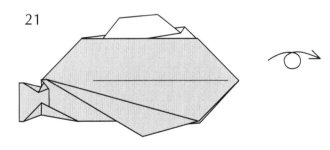

22

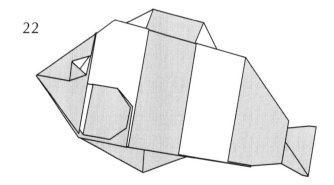

Clown Fish

Animals

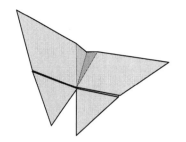

Animals are very lively subjects to fold. Here is a collection of a dozen simple, traditional favorites including the jumping frog, fox puppet, and flying butterfly.

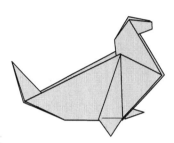

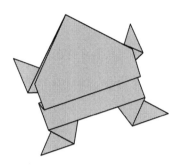

Sitting Fox

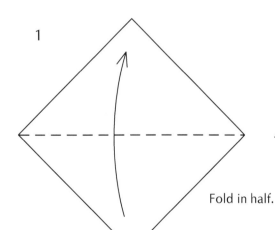

1

Fold in half.

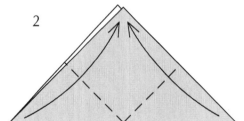

2

Fold the corners up.

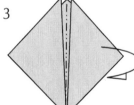

3

Fold behind.

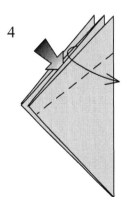

4

Open and rotate.

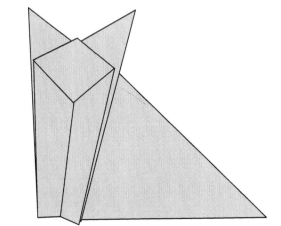

5

Sitting Fox

Dog

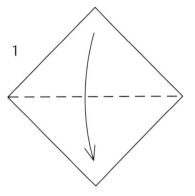

1

Fold in half.

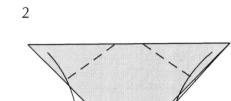

2

Fold the ears down.

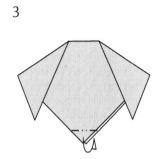

3

Fold behind.

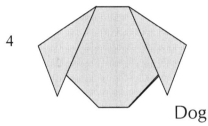

4

Dog

Rabbit

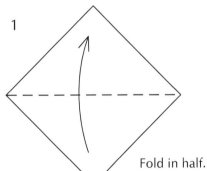

1

Fold in half.

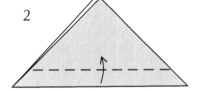

2

3

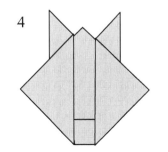

4

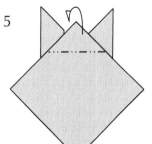

5

Fold behind.

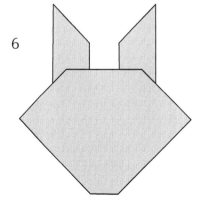

6

Rabbit

Horse

1
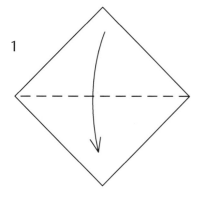

Fold in half.

2
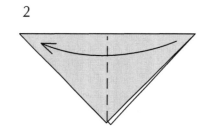

Fold in half.

3
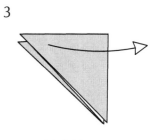

Unfold.

4
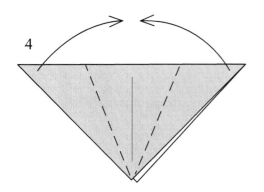

5

Fold the ears behind.

6
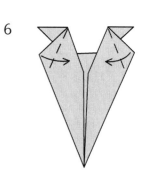

7
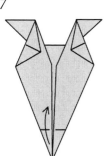

8

9
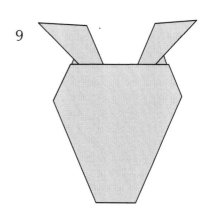

Horse

Cat

1
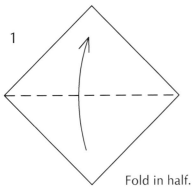

Fold in half.

2
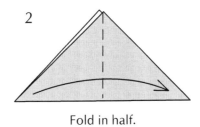

Fold in half.

3
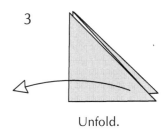

Unfold.

4
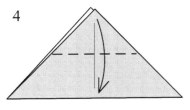

Fold the top layer down.

5
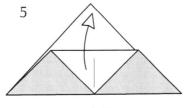

Unfold.

6
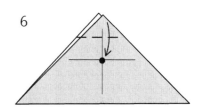

Fold both layers to the dot.

7
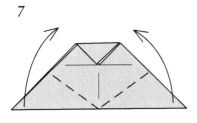

Fold up on both sides.

8
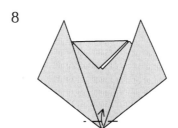

Fold the tip up.

9

10

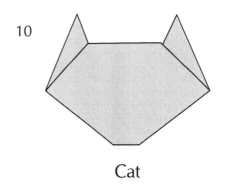

Cat

Fox Puppet

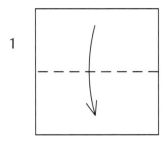

1

Fold in half.

2

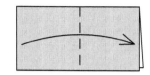

Fold in half.

3

Unfold.

4

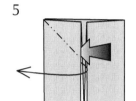

Fold to the center.

5

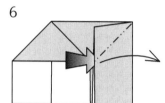

Squash-fold.

6

Squash-fold.

7

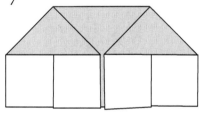

8

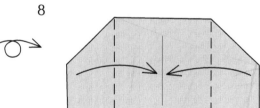

Fold to the center.

9

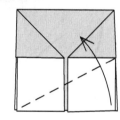

Fold the top layer up
and repeat behind.

10

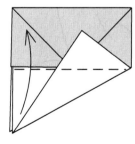

Fold the top layer up and
repeat behind. Rotate 90°.

11

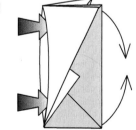

Place your finger and thumb
inside to shape the mouth.

12

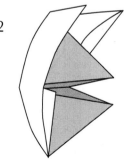

Fox Puppet

Cicada

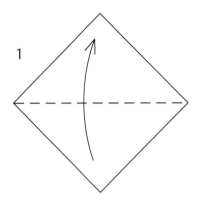

1

Fold in half.

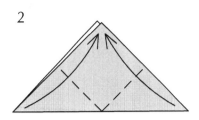

2

Fold the corners up.

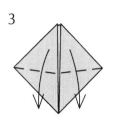

3

Fold the wings down.

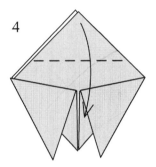

4

Fold the top layer down.

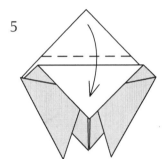

5

Fold down.

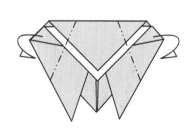

6

Fold behind.

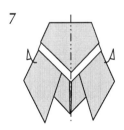

7

Bend in half.

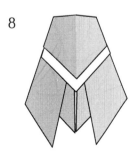

8

Cicada

Butterfly

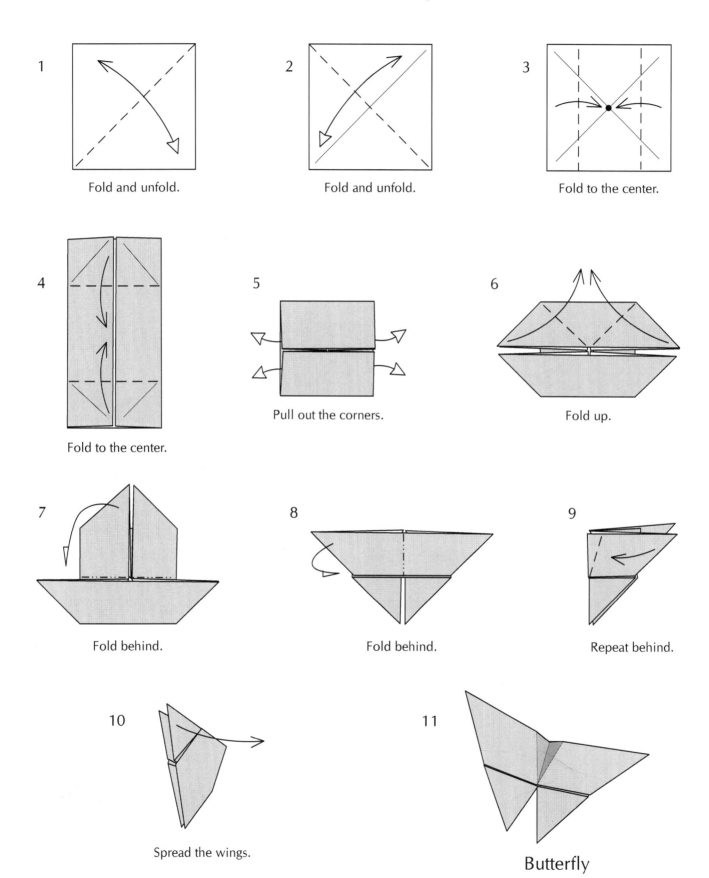

1 Fold and unfold.

2 Fold and unfold.

3 Fold to the center.

4 Fold to the center.

5 Pull out the corners.

6 Fold up.

7 Fold behind.

8 Fold behind.

9 Repeat behind.

10 Spread the wings.

11 Butterfly

Seal

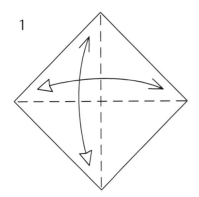

1

Fold and unfold.

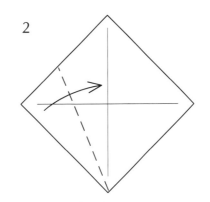

2

Fold to the center.

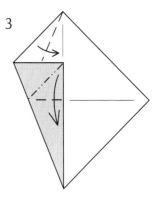

3

Squash-fold.

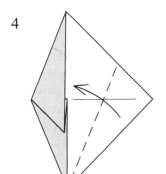

4

Repeat steps 2–3
on the right.

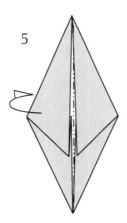

5

Fold in half and rotate.

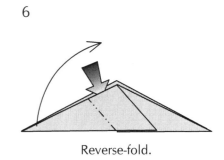

6

Reverse-fold.

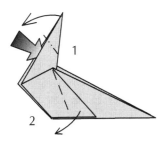

7

1. Reverse-fold.
2. Fold down and
   repeat behind.

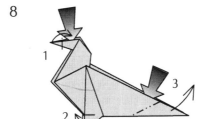

8

1. Reverse-fold.
2. Fold up and
   repeat behind.
3. Reverse-fold.

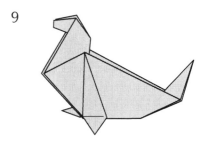

9

Seal

Pig

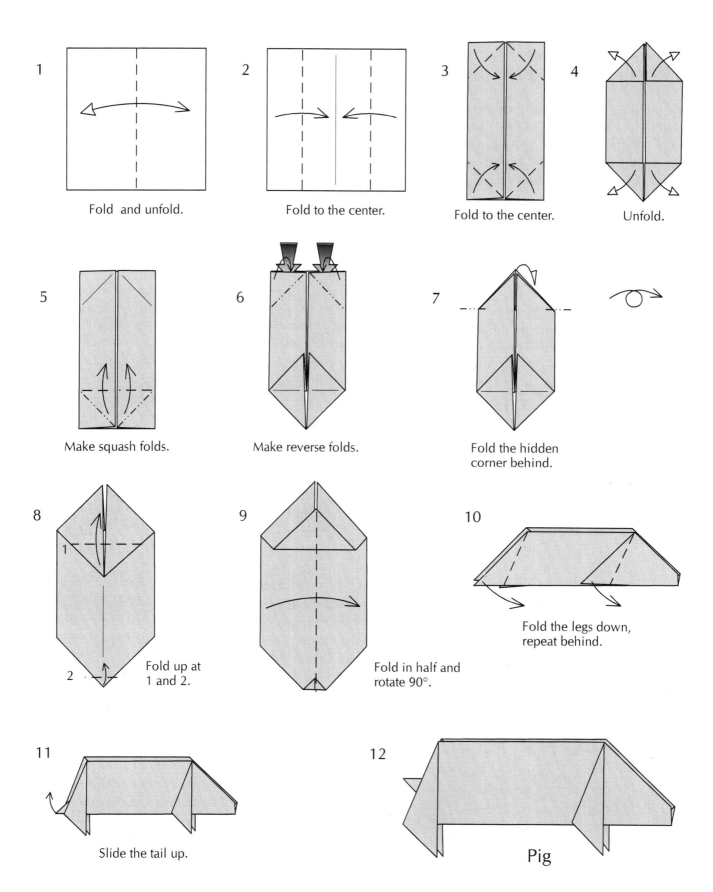

1 Fold and unfold.

2 Fold to the center.

3 Fold to the center.

4 Unfold.

5 Make squash folds.

6 Make reverse folds.

7 Fold the hidden corner behind.

8 Fold up at 1 and 2.

9 Fold in half and rotate 90°.

10 Fold the legs down, repeat behind.

11 Slide the tail up.

12 Pig

Frog

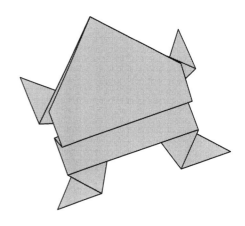

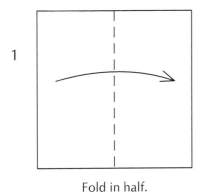

1

Fold in half.

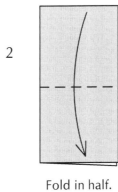

2

Fold in half.

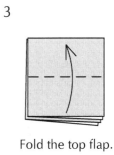

3

Fold the top flap.

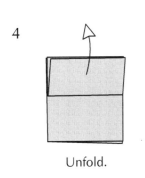

4

Unfold.

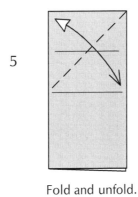

5

Fold and unfold.

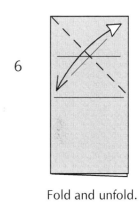

6

Fold and unfold.

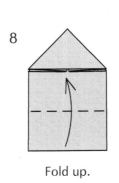

7

Fold along the creases.

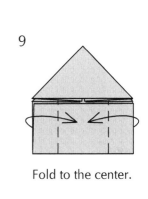

8

Fold up.

9

Fold to the center.

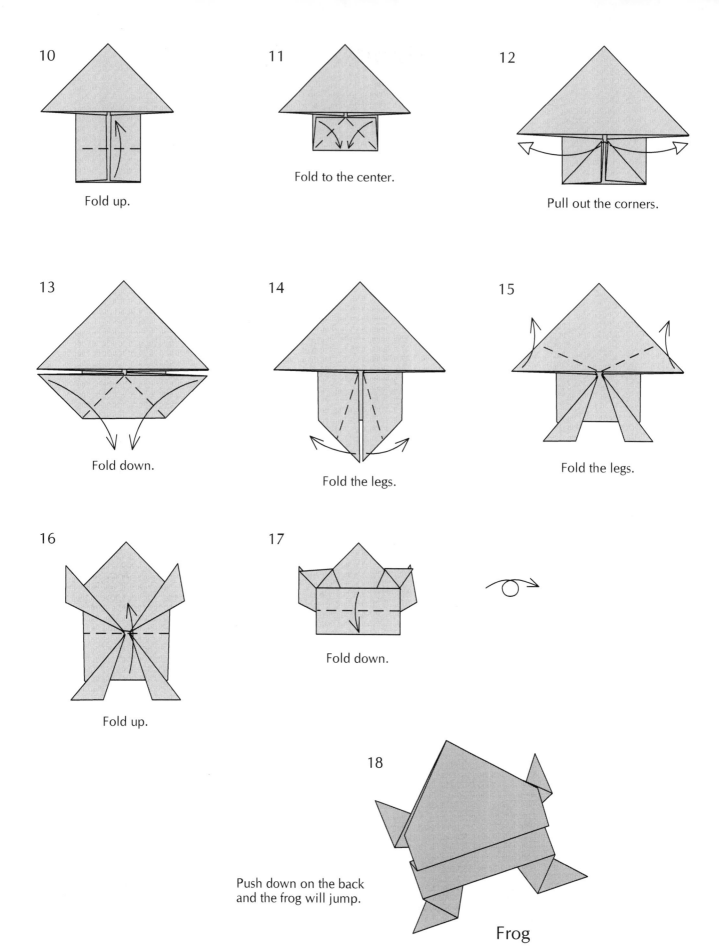

10 Fold up.

11 Fold to the center.

12 Pull out the corners.

13 Fold down.

14 Fold the legs.

15 Fold the legs.

16 Fold up.

17 Fold down.

18 Push down on the back and the frog will jump.

Frog

Bunny

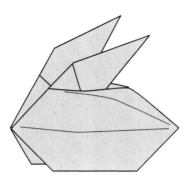

1

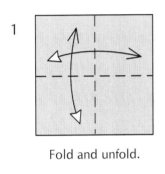

Fold and unfold.

2

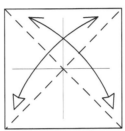

Fold and unfold.

3

Collapse along
the creases.

4

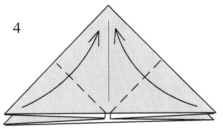

This is the Waterbomb Base.
Fold the corners up in front.

5

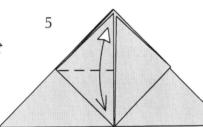

Fold one layer
down and unfold.

6

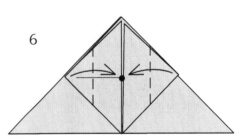

Fold to the center.

7

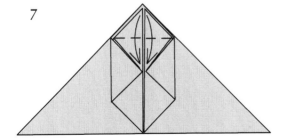

Fold to the center.

8

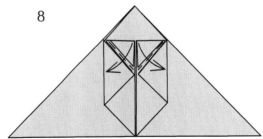

Fold along the edge
of the top layers.

9

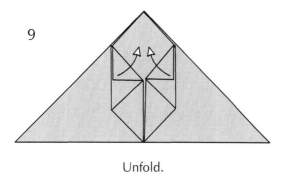

Unfold.

10

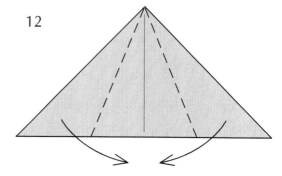

Tuck inside the pockets.

11

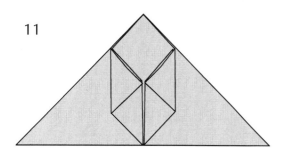

12

Fold to the center.

13

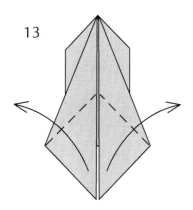

14

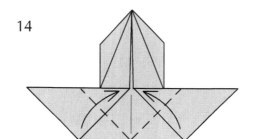

Fold to the center.

15

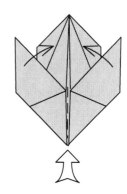

Lift the ears up and
blow into the bottom.

16

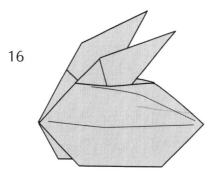

Bunny

People & Plants

Here are some traditional models of people, clothing, and plants. This includes some kimonos and the Japanese wrestlers Fukusuke and Yakko-San.

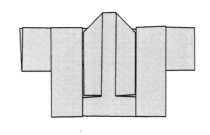
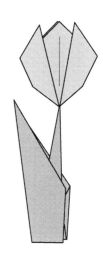

Christmas Tree

1
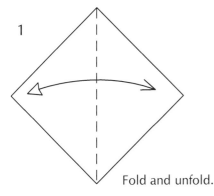
Fold and unfold.

2
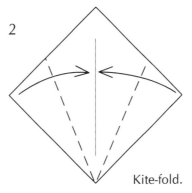
Kite-fold.

3
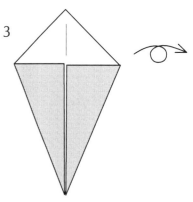

4
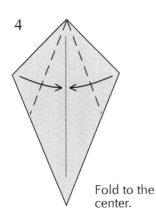
Fold to the center.

5

6
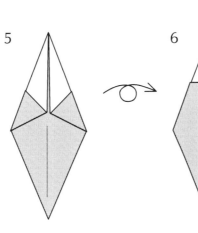
Fold down.
Rotate 180°.

7
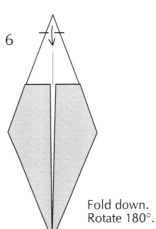
Fold up.

8
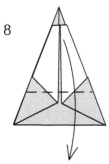
Fold down.

9
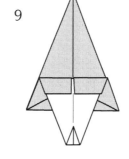

10
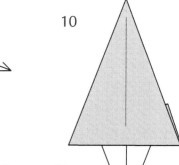
Christmas Tree

Tulip & Stem

Tulip

1

Fold in half.

2

Fold the corners up.

3

Spread the paper.

4

Fold behind.

5

Tulip

The tulip and stem are made from separate sheets of paper. They do not attach but can be used in greeting cards, where they are pasted on the card.

Stem

1

Fold and unfold.

2

Kite-fold.

3

Kite-fold.

4

Kite-fold.

5

Fold up.

6

Fold in half.

7

Slide out.

8

Tulip and Stem

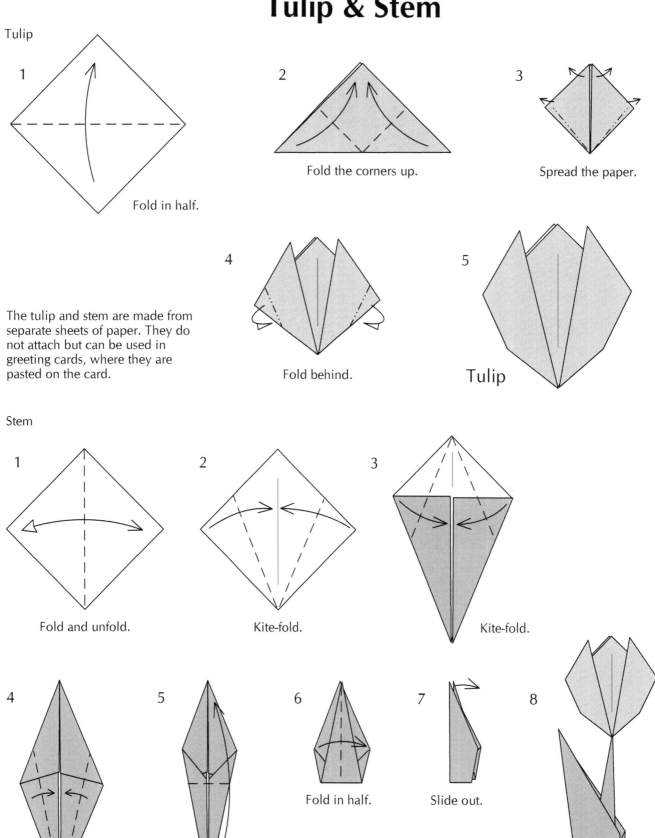

Rose

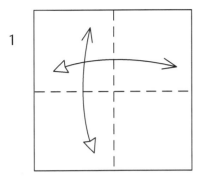

1

Fold and unfold.

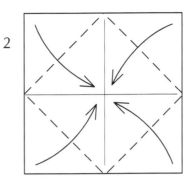

2

Fold to the center.

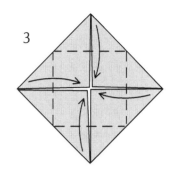

3

Fold to the center.

4

Fold to the center (third time).

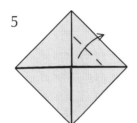

5

Fold the corner beyond the edge.

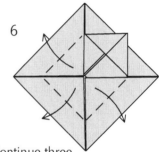

6

Continue three more times.

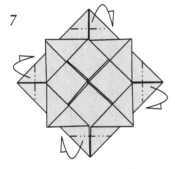

7

Fold the corners behind.

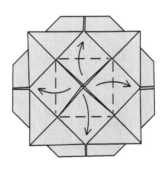

8

Fold the top corners.

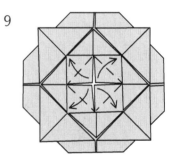

9

Fold the corners.

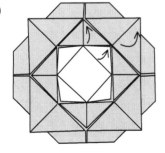

10

Curl all the petals.

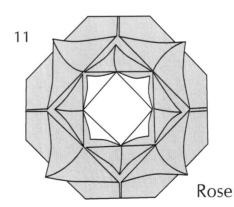

11

Rose

Fukusuke

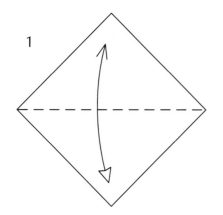

1

Fold and unfold.

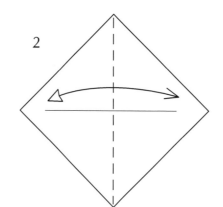

2

Fold and unfold.

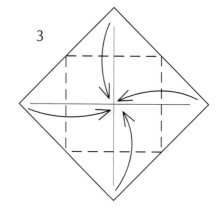

3

Fold the corners
to the center.

4

Fold to the center.

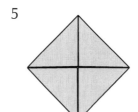

5

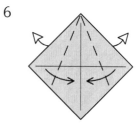

6

Kite-fold and swing the
paper from behind.

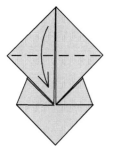

7

Fold down and swing the
paper up from behind.

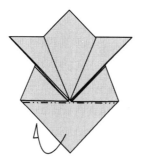

8

Fold behind.

9

Fukusuke

Japanese Sumo Wrestler.

Yakko-San

1

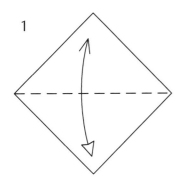

Fold and unfold.

2

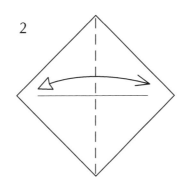

Fold and unfold.

3

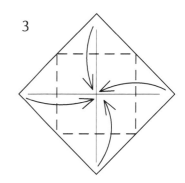

Fold the corners
to the center.

4

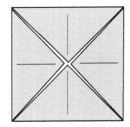

This is the Blintz Fold.

5

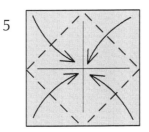

Fold to the center.

6

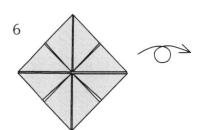

7

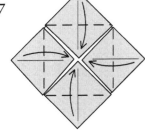

Fold to the center.

8

Turn over and rotate.

9

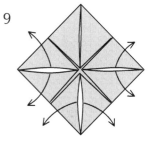

Open on three sides.

10

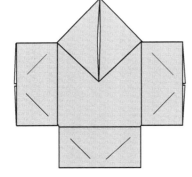

Yakko-San

Wrestler

Kimono

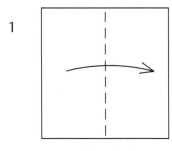

1 Fold in half.

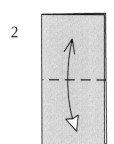

2 Fold and unfold.

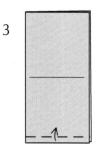

3 Fold a thin strip.

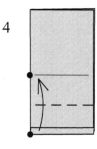

4 Fold the bottom to the crease.

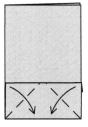

5 Fold to the bottom edge.

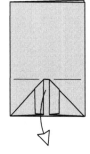

6 Unfold.

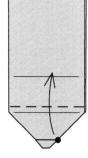

7 Fold up so the dot is slightly above the crease.

8 Fold in half.

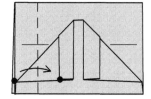

9 The dots will meet.

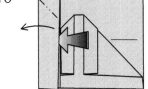

10 Squash-fold.

11 Repeat steps 9–10 on the right.

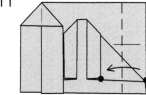

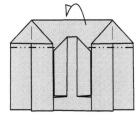

12 Fold behind.

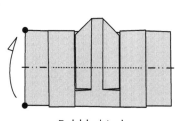

13 Fold behind.

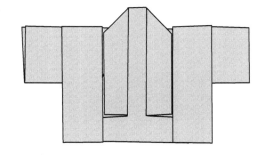

14

Kimono

Tall Kimono

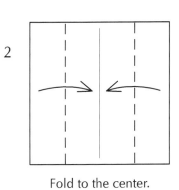

1

Fold and unfold.

2

Fold to the center.

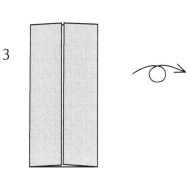

3

4

Fold to the center and swing
the paper out from behind.

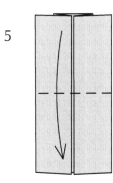

5

Fold in half.

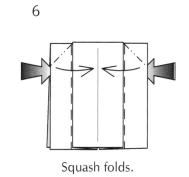

6

Squash folds.

7

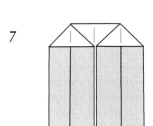

8

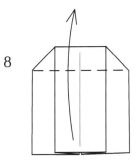

9

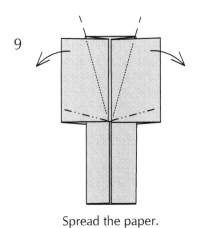

Spread the paper.

10

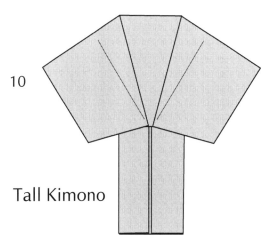

Tall Kimono

Happi Coat

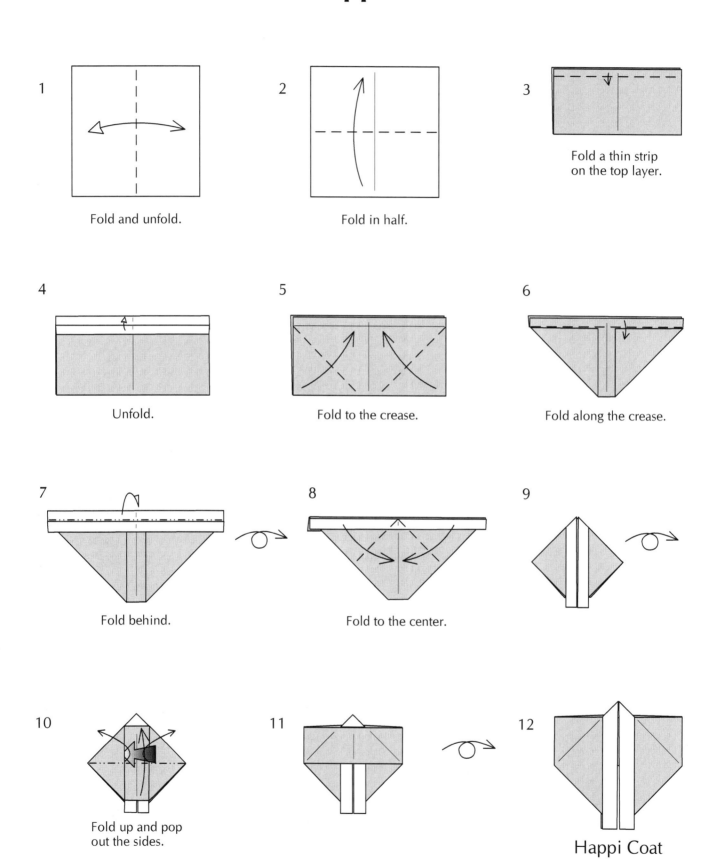

1 Fold and unfold.

2 Fold in half.

3 Fold a thin strip on the top layer.

4 Unfold.

5 Fold to the crease.

6 Fold along the crease.

7 Fold behind.

8 Fold to the center.

9

10 Fold up and pop out the sides.

11

12 Happi Coat

Boxes

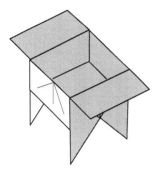
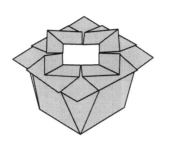
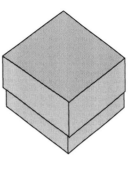
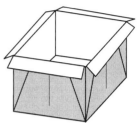

Origami Boxes are simple and fun to make. They are all three-dimensional, come in varied shapes, and all end in a surprising way when the model opens. Here is a collection of a dozen simple, traditional boxes. For the new folder, I would recommend starting with the easiest models. This includes the multibox and oblong box.

Multibox

1
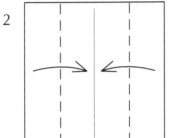

Fold and unfold.

2

Fold to the center.

3

Fold thin strips.

4

Unfold.

5
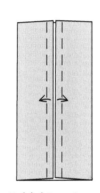
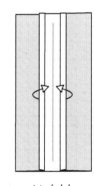

Fold to the creases.

6

Fold along the creases.

7

Open the box.

8

Multibox

Oblong Box

1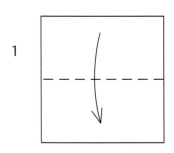

Fold in half.

2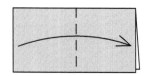

Fold in half.

3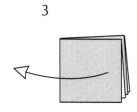

Unfold.

4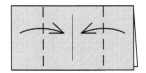

Fold to the center.

5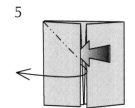

Squash-fold.

6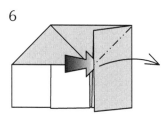

Squash-fold.

7

Repeat behind.

8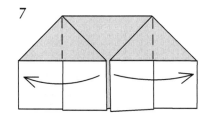

Repeat behind.

9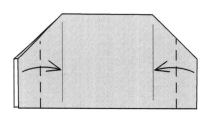

Repeat behind.

10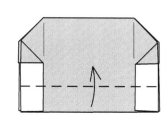

Repeat behind and rotate.

11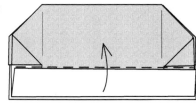

Open the box.

12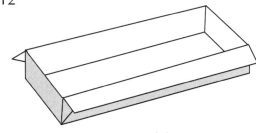

Oblong Box

Box with Lid

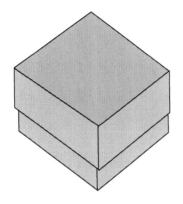

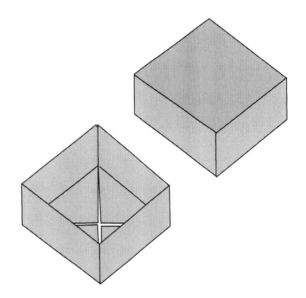

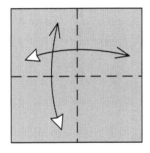

1 Fold and unfold.

2 Fold the corners to the center.

3 Unfold and rotate.

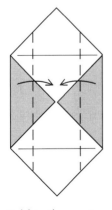

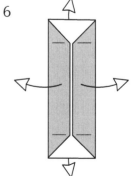

4 Fold to the center.

5 Fold behind.

6 Unfold.

7

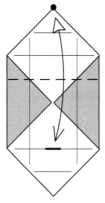

Fold and unfold.

8

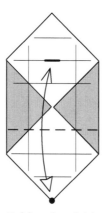

Fold and unfold.

9

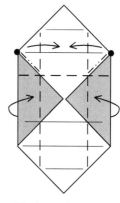

Fold along the creases.
The dots will meet.

10

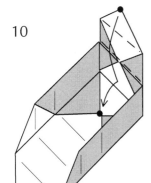

Cover the bottom.
The dots will meet.

11

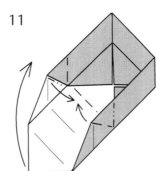

Repeat steps 9–10 in
the other direction.

12

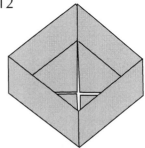

For the lid, fold a
slighly larger box.

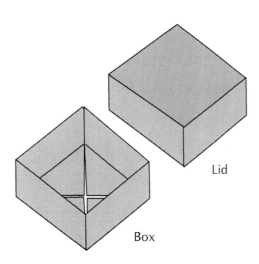

Lid

Box

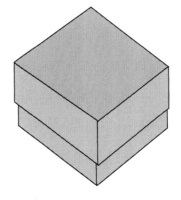

Box with Lid

Christmas Box

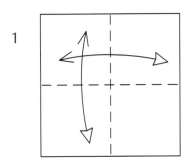

1

Fold and unfold.

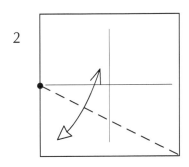

2

Fold and unfold.

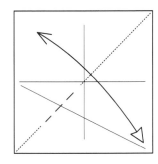

3

Fold and unfold creasing in the lower middle part.

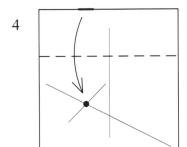

4

Bring the edge to the dot.

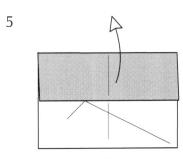

5

Unfold.

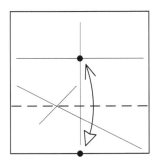

6

Fold and unfold.

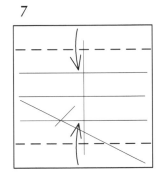

7

8

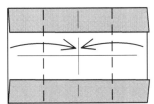

9

Squash-fold.

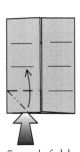

10

Make three more squash folds.

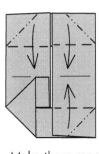

11

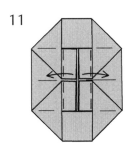

12

Open.

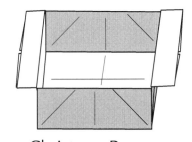

13

Christmas Box

Little Box

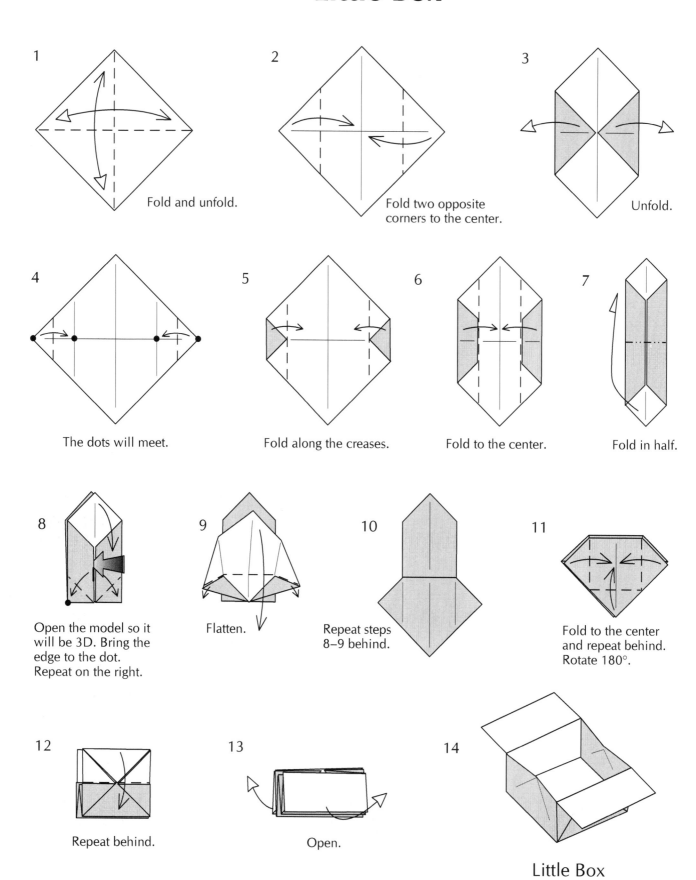

1

Fold and unfold.

2

Fold two opposite
corners to the center.

3

Unfold.

4

The dots will meet.

5

Fold along the creases.

6

Fold to the center.

7

Fold in half.

8

Open the model so it
will be 3D. Bring the
edge to the dot.
Repeat on the right.

9

Flatten.

10

Repeat steps
8–9 behind.

11

Fold to the center
and repeat behind.
Rotate 180°.

12

Repeat behind.

13

Open.

14

Little Box

Gift Box

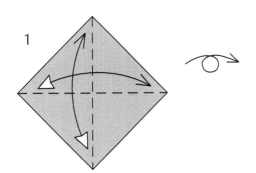

1

Fold and unfold.

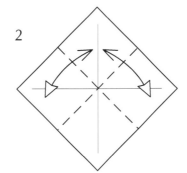

2

Fold and unfold.

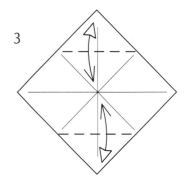

3

Fold and unfold opposite corners to the center.

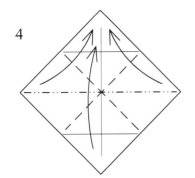

4

Refold along the creases.

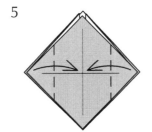

5

Fold to the center. Repeat behind.

6

Fold to the center. Repeat behind.

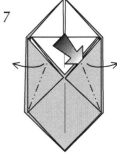

7

Squash folds. Repeat behind.

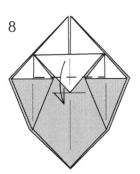

8

Fold down. Repeat behind.

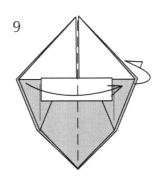

9

Fold the top left flap to the right and repeat behind.

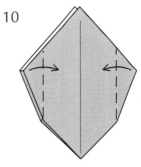

10

Fold towards the center. Repeat behind.

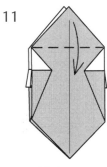

11

Fold down. Repeat behind.

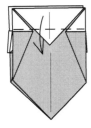

12

Fold down. Repeat behind.

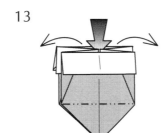

13

Open.

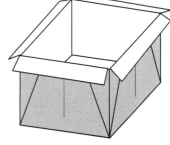

14

Gift Box

Candy Box

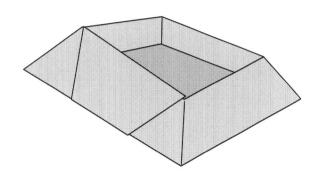

1

Fold and unfold.

2

Fold and unfold.

3

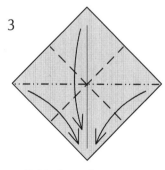

Fold along the creases.

4

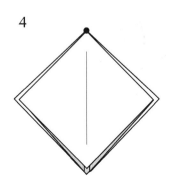

Rotate the dot
to the bottom.

5

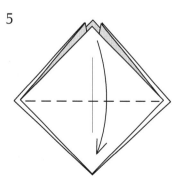

Fold the top layer down
and repeat behind.

6

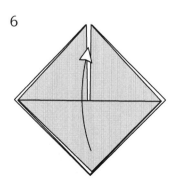

Unfold, repeat
behind.

7

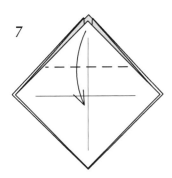

Fold the top layer down
and repeat behind.

8

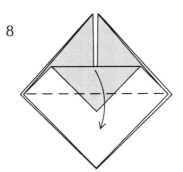

Fold down and
repeat behind.

9

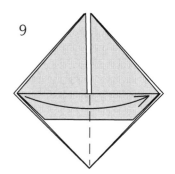

Fold to the right
and repeat behind.

10

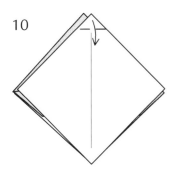

Fold the tip down,
repeat behind.

11

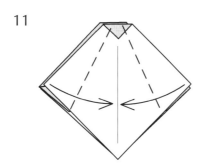

Kite-fold,
repeat behind.

12

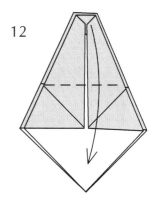

Fold down and
repeat behind.

13

Tuck inside,
repeat behind.

14

Open the box.

15

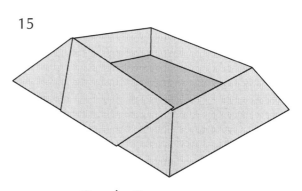

Candy Box

Candy Dish

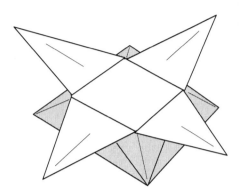

1

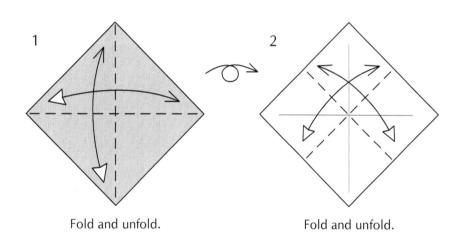

Fold and unfold.

2

Fold and unfold.

3

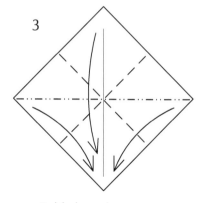

Fold along the creases.

4

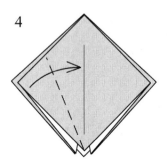

This is the
Preliminary Fold.

5

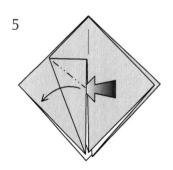

Squash-fold.

6

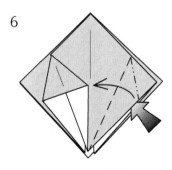

Squash-fold.

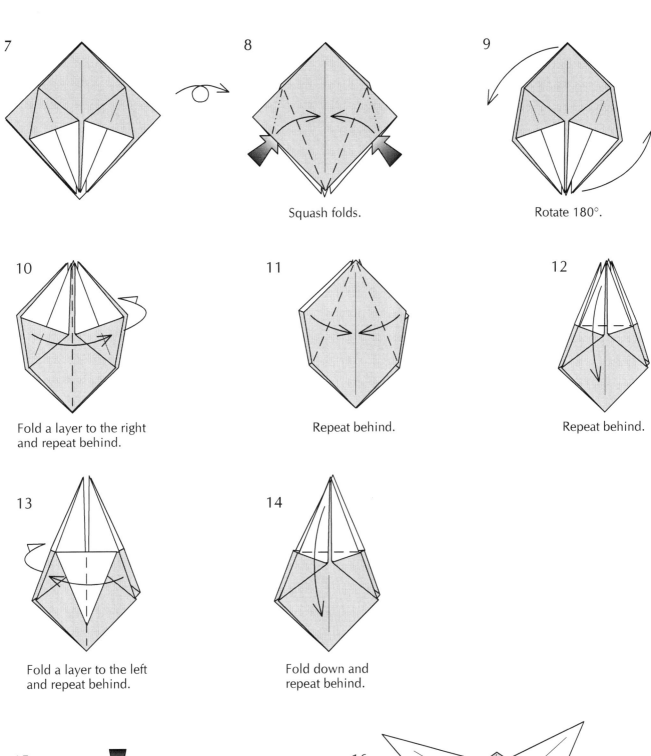

7

8

Squash folds.

9

Rotate 180°.

10

Fold a layer to the right
and repeat behind.

11

Repeat behind.

12

Repeat behind.

13

Fold a layer to the left
and repeat behind.

14

Fold down and
repeat behind.

15

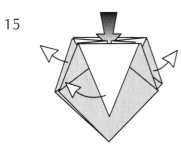

Open and flatten
the bottom.

16

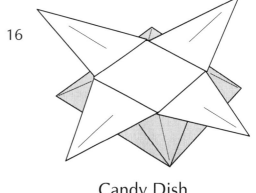

Candy Dish

Sanbow 1

1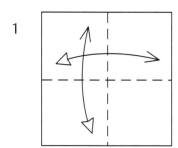

Fold and unfold.

2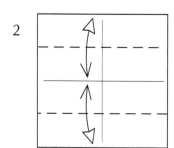

Fold to the center
and unfold.

3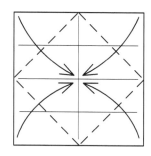

Fold the corners
to the center.

4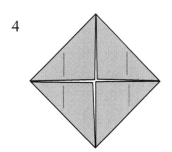

5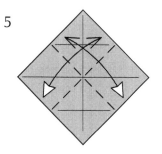

Fold and unfold.

6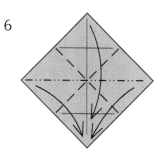

This is the same as
the preliminary fold.

7

Open while folding
up. Repeat behind.

8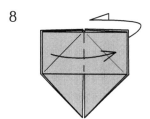

Fold to the right and repeat
behind. Rotate 180°.

9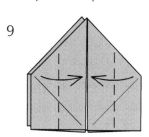

Fold to the center.
Repeat behind.

10

Repeat behind.

11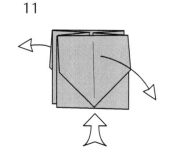

Spread the box.

12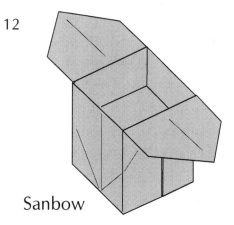

Sanbow

Sanbow 2

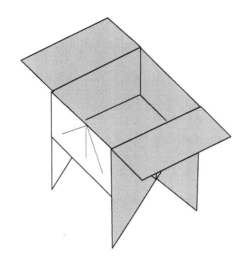

1

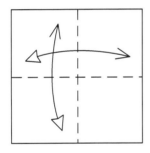

Fold and unfold.

2

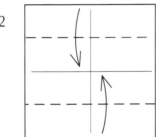

Fold to the center.

3

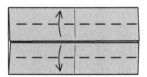

4

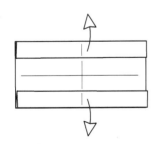

Unfold.

5

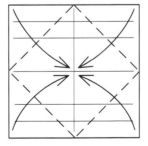

Fold the corners
to the center.

6

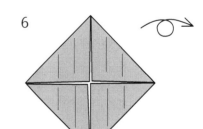

7

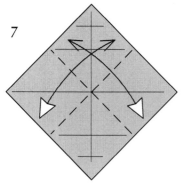

Fold and unfold.

8

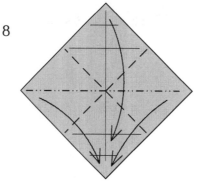

This is the same as
the preliminary fold.

9

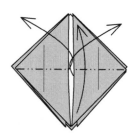

Open while folding
up. Repeat behind.

10

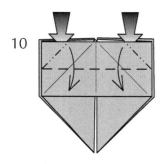

Squash-fold on the left
and right. Repeat behind.

11

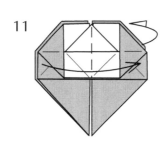

Fold to the right and repeat
behind. Rotate 180°.

12

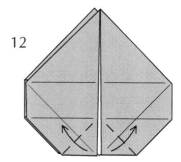

Repeat behind.

13

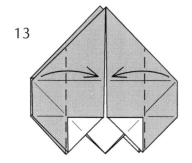

Fold to the center.
Repeat behind.

14

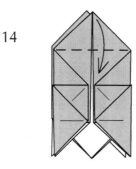

Repeat behind.

15

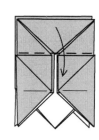

Repeat behind.

16

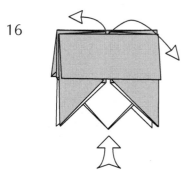

Spread the box.

17

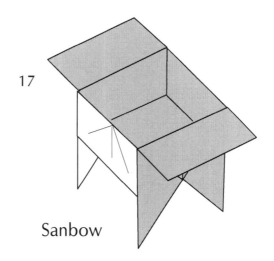

Sanbow

Fancy Box

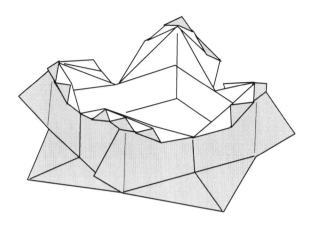

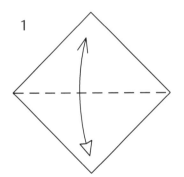

1

Fold and unfold.

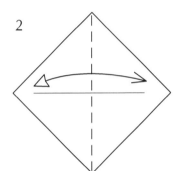

2

Fold and unfold.

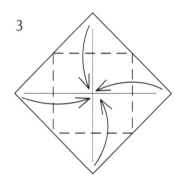

3

Fold the corners
to the center.

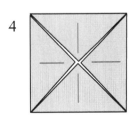

4

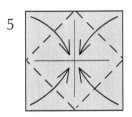

5

Fold the corners
to the center.

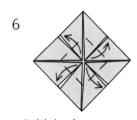

6

Fold the four corners.

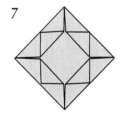

7

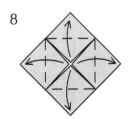

8

Fold the four corners.

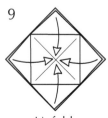

9

Unfold.

10

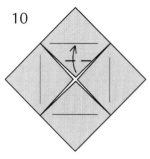

Fold a corner up.

11

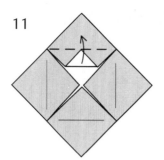

Fold along the crease.

12

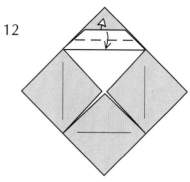

Let the corner slide out.

13

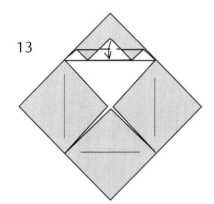

Fold down.

14

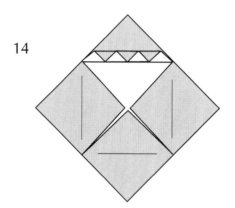

Repeat steps 10–13 on the three sides.

15

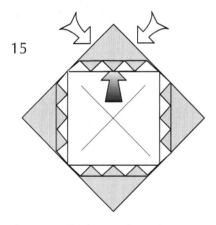

Place your finger inside and push from the outside. Repeat for each side.

16

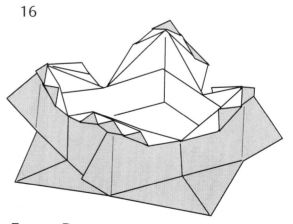

Fancy Box

Chinese Vase

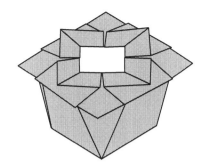

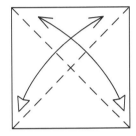

1 Fold and unfold.

2 Fold and unfold.

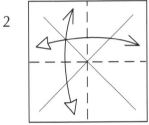

3 Fold and unfold.

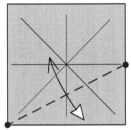

4 Fold to the dot.

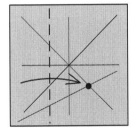

5 Unfold.

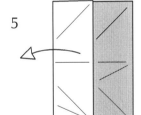

6 Fold and unfold.

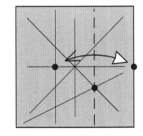

7 Fold and unfold.

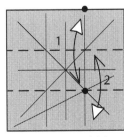

8 Fold and unfold
on four sides.

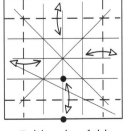

9 Fold to the center.
Mountain-fold along
the creases.

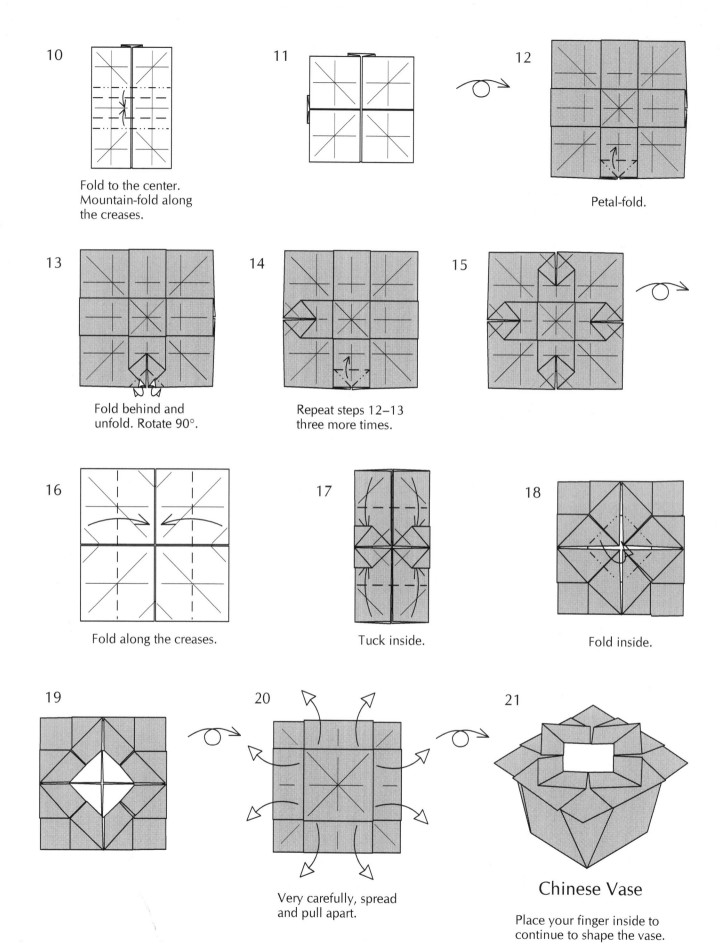

10 Fold to the center.
Mountain-fold along
the creases.

11

12 Petal-fold.

13 Fold behind and
unfold. Rotate 90°.

14 Repeat steps 12–13
three more times.

15

16 Fold along the creases.

17 Tuck inside.

18 Fold inside.

19

20 Very carefully, spread
and pull apart.

21 **Chinese Vase**

Place your finger inside to
continue to shape the vase.

Made in the USA
Charleston, SC
05 September 2012